# THE CROSS-COUNTRY SKI BOOK

# THE CROSS-COUNTRY SKI BOOK

## John Caldwell

### THE STEPHEN GREENE PRESS

Brattleboro, Vermont • Lexington, Massachusetts

## AUTHOR'S ACKNOWLEDGMENT

The generosity of the following people and organizations was prompted by their feeling for cross-country skiing, and I thank them.

None of the skiers whose pictures appear in this book asked for or received any remuneration, gift, or benefit for giving permission to be photographed.

Grateful acknowledgment is also made to A-Foto for photograph 80; to *The Boston Globe* for 96; Canadian Association For Disabled Skiers for 70; Eastern Ski Association for 71; Healthsports for 67; Geordie Heller for halftitle and title page photographs and also 4, 5, 6, 8, 9, 10, 11, 12, 13, 20–23, 24–29, 30–34, 35–40, 41, 42–45, 46–53, 54, 55, 56–60, 61, 74, 75, 78, 79; Ski for Light for 65, 66; Telemark Photo for 1; Bob Woodward for 62, 98, 99. The remaining photographs are mine.

Publishing history of *The Cross-Country Ski Book*

*The Cross-Country Ski Book:* published December 1964, 6 printings through November 1968.
*The Cross-Country Ski Book, 2nd Edition:* published November 1968, 5 printings through November 1971.
*The New Cross-Country Ski Book, 3rd Edition:* published November 1971, 5 printings through December 1973.
*The New Cross-Country Ski Book, 4th Edition:* published December 1973, 7 printings through December 1977. (Bantam Books published November 1976; published as *Le Ski du Fond* by Les Editions de L'Homme, 1974)
*The New Cross-Country Ski Book, 4th Edition:* (indexed) published December 1975, 4 printings through December 1977.
*Cross-Country Skiing Today* (the 5th edition of the work): published December 1977, 8 printings through September 1981 (a selection of the Playboy Book Club, Cooperative Book Service, Quality Paperback Book Club, and Book-of-the-Month Club).
*The Cross-Country Ski Book, 6th Edition* (new format): published October 1981, 4 printings through January 1984.

*Seventh Edition*

Copyright © 1984, 1971, 1973, 1975, 1977, 1981 by John Caldwell

This book is manufactured in the United States of America. It is designed by Irving Perkins Associates and published by The Stephen Greene Press, Fessenden Road, Brattleboro, Vermont 05301.

Distributed in the United States by E.P. Dutton Inc., New York.

**Library of Congress Cataloging in Publication Data**

Caldwell, John H., 1928–
   The cross-country ski book.

   Bibliography: p.
   Includes index.
   1. Cross-country skiing. I. Title.
GV855.3.C34    1984     796.93     84–13588
ISBN 0-8289-0544-4 (pbk.)

# CONTENTS

# INTRODUCTION

IT'S BEEN TWENTY YEARS since I wrote the first book on x-c. That relic had six chapters (six, count 'em!), 80 pages, and lots of pictures. I had to haul up short in the first chapter, entitled "What Is It?" and describe the sport. The other chapters contained information on equipment, technique, training, waxing, and joys of. Since then a lot has been written about x-c. In fact, there are specialty books on material covered in each of the original chapters in my book. The sport has grown rapidly, the ski industry is taking serious note of it, and there is much more to say. That's for sure.

While the causes for all this are gratifying, the wealth of material itself can be a bit mind-boggling. It's easy to get side-tracked and lose sight of the basics in this sport. With 3.5 million x-c skiers in the country alone, according to one estimate, there is room for several different approaches to the sport, or opinions on anything to do with the sport. Few activities have been so subjected to the umbrella effect. Now many people associate with cross-country skiing the following: backpacking on skis, ski-mountaineering, Telemarking, and downhill cross-country skiing. Still others decry the use of tracks for skiing, complain about the crowds saying the sport used to be so nice when it was lonely out there, and so on.

I'm not eager to get into arguments with anyone about semantics, or the sport itself. Or even claim what the sport really is, or should be. That's up to you to decide. But I really have made an effort to try and keep things simple.

Occasionally I give talks to junior skiers at racing camps and lately my favorite has been The Seven-Minute Talk. I claim to tell young racers, in seven minutes or less, 95 to 98 percent of what they need to know. When I get to the equipment section of my talk, for instance, I tell them to make sure the curved part of the ski is pointing forward. The point is that there are a lot of good racing skis on the market and rather than

**1.** *The '84 start of America's most popular touring race, the Birkebeiner, at Telemark, Wisconsin.*

spend time worrying about all the flexes and measurements they would be better off skiing or training. After one delivery I was followed on the program by a sports medicine doctor who had graphs and diagrams covering anaerobic threshold, oxygen uptake, and all those high falutin' things. He swore quietly at me before he started saying I had set skiing back ten years with my simple approach. Of course I didn't believe him then and I don't believe him now.

I don't need to know the chemical formula for the base on my skis. I'm happy enough ignorant of this information. In fact, I don't even know why I feel so good after exercise. I know it works and that's good enough for me.

So, in short, I've tried to glean from the material available and have presented what I consider the 95 percent of it for the kind of x-c skiing I do. Just about. I admit to being a maverick when it comes to technique and even after 30 years of coaching I still find new approaches to this fascinating subject. My coaching colleagues just shake their heads when they hear some of my theories and I may have gone off the deep end here. You be the judge.

I often refer to the U.S. Ski Team. I have been a member of that team,

**2.** *The Olympic flags marking the cross-country venue at Sarajevo, Yugoslavia, in February, 1984*

**3.** *Biathlon is an increasingly popular sport stemming from cross-country. Here a U.S. skier starts the 10 km race at the 1984 Sarajevo Olympics.*

and have been coaching it or members of it, since 1952 and have formed some of my fondest associations with this group. These skiers have set so many worldwide trends in x-c that anyone would be remiss in not recognizing them or referring to them. For instance, the U.S. skiers were among the first to begin using fiberglass skis for racing; they were the first to introduce hotwaxing of the tips and tails; they were the big influence in putting an element of Alpine skiing ability into x-c racing; they were instrumental in introducing the use of waxless skis of all varieties in racing and they were instrumental in bringing the marathon skate to racing from the tour-race circuit. It's been a privilege to work with these skiers. The information I pass on to you is something I think many of you can benefit from. This group even shows it is human by goofing up once in a while and I have written a little bit about this.

This thing referred to as cross-country skiing is a marvelous sport, mainly because it attracts so many different people with so many different interests. Some go out for the exercise, some for the peace and tranquillity of it, some for the challenge, some to be out-of-doors, some to race, some because it's the "in" thing, some because of the fashions and new equipment, some to socialize, some to Telemark, backpack, downhill ski or break out new tracks in the powder, and some to be alone. Well, have fun at it and remember, keep the curved part in front of you.

# THE CROSS-COUNTRY SKI BOOK

1

# Equipment

THE MOST APPARENT CHANGE in x-c skiing is in the equipment area. It's a big business now and ski trade journals devote pages to the coverage of x-c equipment. You can hear or read arguments for various ski constructions, different materials, different lengths, widths, flexes, and so on. It's mind-boggling and I have stopped trying to keep up with it all. But a few things don't seem to change and I am fairly sure that the tenets I list below will hold during the next few years. After that I'll describe the present equipment scene.

1. *It's safe to say that equipment manufacturers are out to make money,* and therefore you can expect them to exert pressures, however subtle, to get you to buy new equipment every season or two.
2. *New equipment will continue to appear each year.* But if your present equipment works well, stick with it until it wears out—unless *you* want to change. Remember, this is your sport and you do it the way you want to.
3. *There are so many different skis available these days that you can be assured of getting what you want if you look around long enough.* You can find manufacturers who produce Telemark skis, backpacking or backcountry models, wide touring skis, narrower touring skis, racing skis, cross-country downhill skis—you name it. And almost every company makes waxless and waxable skis. You can begin to get a picture of the different possibilities. This leads into. . . .
4. *If you need some new equipment, take the time to test different models.* Determine where you will do most of your skiing, what kind of skiing you will be doing, and go on from there. You might be wise to rent skis for a time, or borrow some from a friend, just to be able to test their skis' characteristics.

3

Since most of my skiing is done in tracks as a coach, I always use racing skis. But even if I am breaking out tracks I can use these in the East since we don't get many deep snowfalls. And when spring touring comes around we can ski on top of the snow anyway, so the racing models work fine.

If I lived in an area where there was a lot of deep powder I'm sure I would use wider skis much of the time, especially on tours.

5. *Wood skis are becoming quite scarce and if you have some you are attached to you had better take good care of them.* The x-c industry is following the pattern established by the Alpine people several years ago. I began my skiing career on wood Alpine skis. I even started x-c on Alpine ski cut-downs, those marvelous exhibits with the sections containing the steel edges trimmed off to make a narrow, at that time sleek-looking, x-c ski.

6. *More and more recreational skiers are switching to narrower x-c skis.* This is especially true for competent skiers who have access to track skiing.

7. *Cross-country downhill skis are an important item on the market at present.* These skis are a cross between touring skis and Alpine skis, being wider than most touring skis, yet narrower than most Alpine skis. They also have edges and are particularly well-suited for skiing downhill. Some people claim the addicts of this sport may want better per-formance in their Alpine skiing and then go to Alpine equip-ment, or they may want better performance in their touring and then turn to touring equipment. On the other hand, they may stay content the way they are, especially since they can do their Telemarking with these skis and the proper boots and bindings.

I am not going into these skis below.


## THE SKIS

In getting new equipment your most important decision will be in choosing between waxable and waxless skis.

### Waxable or Waxless?

Waxable skis require—well—waxing. They are the traditional ones, for most of the older people who know x-c.

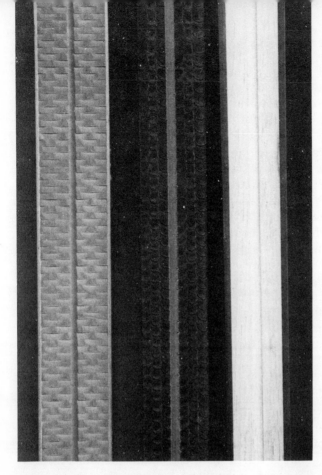

*4. Three different x-c skis. Left, a waxless mountain ski with steel edges. Middle, a waxless touring ski. Right, a real (!) light wooden touring ski with lignostone edges.*

If you are a good waxer, or if you enjoy waxing, or if you want to learn about waxing, you will probably be happier with waxable skis. Compared to waxless skis, most of the time you can get better skiing with waxable skis because well-waxed skis are generally faster and climb more efficiently than their waxless counterparts do.

But the ski manufacturers are working very hard at perfecting new models of waxless skis; perhaps in the near future they will come up with something that even beats the waxable type. As soon as they can market a ski bottom that changes its characteristics according to temperatures and moisture content of the snow they will be closer to providing the flexibility you get with different kinds of wax. Until then, I think you can expect well-waxed skis to carry the day in most conditions.

There isn't much doubt that kids, or beginners, are best off with waxless skis. They are the easiest for them and I recommend them highly.

The disadvantages of waxable skis should be clear: They require waxing, perhaps every time you go skiing. The process takes time and the wax costs money. In addition, waxing is something of an art and not everyone can master its details.

I have compromised, in a way, and have "built" my own waxless skis using an old pair of waxables. I describe this method below.

### THE CHALLENGE OF WAXABLES

I enjoy waxing x-c skis as much as anyone around. I began fooling around with wax in the 1940's and probably will keep at it until I quit skiing. I feel that waxing is a part of the sport, that it adds to the challenges. Cross-country wouldn't be the same to me without it.

O.K., maybe I'm prejudiced. I especially love to wax and go out for a spin around my Vermont neighborhood to see if I can get through all the various snow conditions without having my ski bottoms ice up. In the spring, waxing often poses a problem because the south slopes are warmed and the north slopes may still be powdery. I go ahead and wax anyway, enjoying that expectancy or suspense while I wonder how my wax will work. Some places I am forced to use slightly different techniques, being careful not to lift the skis; in other sections I might have to stomp the skis down hard in order to set the wax. But if I hit the wax right, and make these adjustments in technique, I can ski happily in most of the terrain.

### CONSTRUCTION OF WAXABLES

Waxable skis basically come in two materials—wood and fiberglass. Some fiberglass skis are made entirely of synthetic materials and some have bits and pieces of wood in them. The importance of the fiberglass or other synthetics in a ski is this: Fiberglass makes the skis stronger and less breakable; the fiberglass, or synthetic, bottom surface is stronger, tougher, faster, and more water-resistant than wood; the synthetic materials allow a more uniform—even a programmed—method of construction. Top racers tell the factories exactly how stiff they want their skis under the foot, just ahead of the foot, in the tip, and so on. And they get them that way.

Much as I have used wood x-c skis, and lovely as they are, today I must—shedding a tear or two—vote for the synthetic-materials construction. But the wood skis, being slower, offer an advantage to many people who are not interested in speed. In fact, they welcome some skis that make them feel more comfortable on downhill sections.

## The Waxless Ones

Companies produce two kinds of so-called waxless skis, basically.

There are those that you never wax in order to get climb, purchase, grip, or whatever you want to call it. These include skis with machined patterns, or designs, in their bottoms. The reason you don't wax them is that waxing would interfere with the performance of the ski by clogging the section of the ski that is intended to prevent backslipping.

And there are those waxless skis that you may wax. Understand that you don't have to wax them, but the manufacturers are suggesting that in certain conditions you will be better off with some wax.

You shouldn't think that the manufacturers of the "waxable waxless" skis have failed in comparison to the manufacturers of the pure waxless skis. On the contrary, my vote goes for the "waxable waxless" for the following reasons: No waxless ski works well in all conditions and so if you can't wax it on occasion, you will not always have a good ski. The waxables provide more flexibility. Next, using "waxable waxless" skis will offer you the chance for an introduction to waxing. As I said earlier, waxed skis still outperform waxless models in almost all conditions and the day may come when you switch over.

The main reason for having a waxless ski is to get grip without having to wax. This means that you can go skiing regularly without going through the folderol of waxing.

The speed of the waxless ski is a secondary consideration right now. It has to be, mainly because the manufacturers haven't come up with a really fast waxless ski and therefore cannot make claims in this area. So make no mistake about it, you sacrifice some speed with waxless skis. Nevertheless most users of waxless skis are willing to give this up. In fact, I know lots of tourskiers who like their skis a bit slow on the downhill.

All waxless skis are made basically with synthetic materials, although some contain wood in their innards. However, your choice isn't between wood and synthetic here, but instead is a matter of opting for a particular bottom—and I'll get to these in just a minute.

Despite my personal feelings about waxable vs waxless skis, I think waxless skis are great. They are providing thrills for many newcomers to the sport. There is no question that waxing can be difficult and that many skiers are turned off by it. (My waxable-ski friends in the midwest are spoiled by their powder snow conditions and when klister skiing comes in the spring they tell me that many of them hang 'em up for the season. They can't stand klister waxing. Whereas, if we didn't use klister in the East we'd do precious little skiing.)

The main drawback to waxless skis has already been alluded to, and it's a mechanical thing. The bottoms on the pure waxless skis are a given, a fixed. They can not change according to snow conditions. So, most days they work well, some days they don't work quite so well, and some days they don't work well at all.

## The U.S. Ski Team and Waxless Skis—The "Hairies"

In the 1976 Winter Olympics at Seefeld, Austria, 30-km silver medalist Bill Koch used skis with mohair while running the third leg of the 4× 10 relay race. The conditions were ideal for mohair. The tracks in the stadium at the start were very glazed, the temperature was near freezing, but as the course reached the higher northern slopes the snow was much drier. Many skiers using conventional fiberglass racing skis and conventional wax—whatever "conventional wax" could be for these conditions!—iced up on the course and had to stop and de-ice before finishing. Koch had an outstanding time on his leg and thereby really put mohair skis on the map.

A few years later a Norwegian racer won a medal in the prestigious Holmenkollen 50 km race using Fischer Crown skis, another waxless ski with a machined design in the bottom.

There weren't many other unusual results attributed to waxless skis until 1982 at the Swedish Ski Games in Falun. Led by Jim Galanes, members of the U.S. Team began making their own waxless skis at this meet. The waxing conditions were tough, with new snow falling and temperatures around freezing. The racers took a Sandvik tool and roughed up the kicker zone of some clean skis, applied some silicone to prevent drag and icing, and went out and raced. Galanes was so excited with his good wax job that he ran himself into the ground and had to retire, even though he was probably leading the race. The boys with cooler heads, Bill Koch and Dan Simoneau, paced themselves and finished 1–2 in this historic event. Koch went on to win the World Cup that year.

An effort was made to keep the procedure for making these waxless skis under wraps until just recently. Now everyone on the international racing circuit has probably tried Hairies or has a pair in his ski bag. It gets its name "Hairies" from the look of the ski bottoms after they have been roughed up. (It has also been called the "Gismo" wax job.)

The method has already been described, it's so simple. Just get hold of a tool like the Sandvik #400 or a Stanley Surform pocket plane and scratch or scrape away lengthwise on the kicker zone of a clean pair of skis. Cover the roughed surface with some sort of silicone or liquid glider wax, let it dry, and go out and try it. Under normal conditions the job may last for 50–100 km of skiing. I recommend being conservative at the beginning and scraping a short kicker zone and keeping it not too rough. You can always lengthen the zone and make it rougher in order to get more purchase.

You can wax over your Hairies job, and you can use a sharp metal scraper to smooth up the bottoms on your skis again. There is just one problem with doing a Hairies job over and over again. Eventually you will wear away all of the ski bottom and will be down to the innards of the ski. But if you are careful it will take a long, long time. I've been at it for about four years and haven't begun to see through the base of my skis.

I put aside an old pair of my skis that I use for this. They are always ready and I don't have to waste any time choosing wax, or working on skis when these conditions arise.

5. *Roughing up a plain plastic bottom with a Sandvik tool to make a "Hairy."*

6. *A "Hairy" bottom on the right, compared to a mate.*

This is just another example of the innovations brought in by the U.S. Ski Team. It has been primarily responsible for the surge in glide waxing the tips and tails of skis, the manufacture of Hairies, and the introduction of the marathon skate. Skiers all around the world use these techniques now, and believe it or not, many of them recognize their origins.

## WAXLESS BOTTOMS AND HOW THEY WORK

In broad terms, there are two different bottom surfaces on waxless skis. Some manufacturers might insist that their brand deserves a special category, but I'll stick with my arbitrary two in order to keep things simple at this stage.

### MACHINED BOTTOMS

The main type of waxless ski contains steps, many small ridges, diamonds, or some other configurations on the bottom surface. These features help the ski from slipping back when it is pressed into the snow, and they are an integral part of the bottom surface. (The technical-minded people in the industry have further classified these bottoms as being "positive-base" or "negative-base" skis according to whether the steps, etc., protrude from the bottom or are incised in the bottom.)

The most notable variety in this category is the fishscale bottom. Made to resemble overlapping discs, this was the first construction used in manufacturing waxless skis. Today it is probably found on more waxless skis than any other bottom.

It is interesting that the fishscale construction was originally used on Alpine skis in an effort to make them faster. I know that some of the skiers testing these fishscale models were amazed at how well they could ski on them—*uphill*. The idea was sold and patented and now the fishscale is used solely on x-c skis. The other designs, such as diamonds, ridges, steps, etc., are used by different companies who do not hold the fishscale patent.

## The Second Type; All Others

So far, the rest of the waxless skis defy categorizing, unless they might be distinguished by their smoother-looking bottoms. The "waxable waxless" skis have this characteristic, but so do some other pure waxless skis— ones you should not wax under the foot. The key is to find out from your dealer just how the skis should be treated.

These skis may be difficult to break into groups, but it's almost impossible to tell you how they all work.

One of the early types, the mica-based ski, worked on a mechanical principle. Bits of mica were embedded in the base in such a way that they provided grip for the skier. These skis could also be waxed, but great care had to be taken when cleaning them. Scraping the bottoms, for instance, would tend to wear off the mica and make the ski less effective.

There no doubt will be new waxless skis on the market, and some of them will have smooth-looking bottoms, and it will probably be a good idea to stay away from scraping any of these—just as a general rule. Use a wax solvent.

## Technical Points in Choosing a Ski

The many different types of waxless skis present, to me, a certain irony. For, the minute anyone begins to study all the waxless skis and the variables that affect their performance, the subject can get as complicated, or more so, than waxing. The original idea of waxless skis was to have something simple that worked without waxing, right?

Well, you don't really have to know how the waxless skis work, but it is interesting that many of the theories behind them also apply to waxing. If you ask yourself the questions I list below it might help you to pick out a pair of waxless skis that is well suited to you—and you'll have the beginnings of some waxing theory, too.

### IN CONSIDERING MACHINED BOTTOMS

How close together should the steps, etc., be? The more steps, the more ridges to hold against slipping—but the more friction, too.

How deep should the steps be? The deeper they are the more hold you will get. But again, deep steps will cause the skis to be slower on the flats and downhills.

Should the steps be positive—that is, protruding from the running surface of the ski? Or negative—that is, incised into the running surface? Generally, the positive steps grip better, but are also slower than the negative designs.

Should the cuts or steps be graduated so they are deeper under the foot where more force is exerted, and shallower fore and aft of this section?

How much of the running surface should the steps cover?

The answers to all these questions depend on the flex of the ski, the depth of the cuts, the way you ski, and so on.

In most cases you won't have much to do with determining how the manufacturers build their skis, but you can be sure that they are continually experimenting with different types.

### IN CONSIDERING THE OTHERS

These skis have not been tested as long as many of the other waxless varieties, and no doubt new ones will appear on the market. You should find out, before purchasing, if what makes the ski work will wear out with skiing. Can the bottom be waxed? Scraped? Heated?

## HOW EASY TO REPAIR?

One important factor in choosing a waxless ski is its "repairability." If you use your skis enough, and if snow conditions are very harsh, some bottoms will wear out and need replacing. Some bottoms are more easily replaced than others. A few companies service their products; others do not. Check with your shop when you make your purchase.

## SNOW CONDITIONS IN YOUR AREA

It's no secret that we have many different snow conditions in North America, ranging from a little cold powder for a short time to lots of heavy, wet snow for long periods of time. In any event, the conditions in your area might be stable for most of the winter, and in that event, there are probably some waxless skis which will work better, more often, than others. Inquire of your shop, or friends, then get them.

## For Beginner, Intermediate, Expert

I highly recommend waxless skis for beginners. However, I cannot recommend one variety over another. If you are just starting you have the opportunity to try different models. Visit a touring area and rent some equipment. Check with friends to see if they have some skis you can try. Then, if you can determine which skis work best for you in the conditions prevalent in your area, go out and buy a pair.

If you are an intermediate skier who is gaining interest in x-c, and enjoys waxing, you ought to have two pairs of skis, one waxable and one waxless. Then when a situation comes up where the waxing is difficult, or you're in a hurry, you can use the waxless jobs. Other times you can wax and be well off. And there's nothing wrong with having that extra pair of skis for a friend who might go out with you.

For experts, again I would recommend having two pairs of skis, one waxless and one waxable. But I'd make my own waxless skis from an old pair of waxables. That way I would know the ski's flex and could determine the length of my kicker zone when I "fixed" the bottoms. I think, though, that you'll use the waxless skis only when the waxing conditions are extremely difficult. For the present and until the waxless skis are much improved, you will get the best ride on a well-waxed ski. If you are in a hurry to go skiing you will have to decide whether you want to take the time to wax and have a good ski, or not wax and have a bit more time to ski on waxless skis—but at a different speed, or pace.

## Ski Lengths

The old reliable standard still holds: To measure the ski length correct for you, stand on the floor and reach up with your hand. The tip of the ski should come to your wrist.

If you are light for your height, you can go either of two ways in picking out a pair of skis. One is to look for a ski that is relatively soft, or flexible. The other is to get a ski that is slightly shorter; for example, if you measure for a 205-centimeter length, get a 200-cm ski.

It then follows that if you are heavy for your height you should look for a stiffer pair of skis. This is preferable to getting a slightly longer pair, although you might have to go for the extra length in order to get the correct flex.

Kids can manage wonderfully with shorter skis than prescribed above. If the skis are as long as the kid is tall, don't worry. The shorter ones will be easier to learn on, too.

## Tests for Flexibility

With so many different kinds of waxable and waxless skis on the market it is important, and possible, to find some that are the right flex for you. Having the right flex means that the skis will work well. When you wax them correctly you will be able to set the wax, get good purchase, and use good technique to motor along the flats and uphills. And when you use the waxless skis you will be able to get good purchase with them.

If the skis are too stiff you are likely to have difficulty and slip more than you should.

Don't be led astray by judging the skis' camber alone. While camber and flexibility are somewhat related, testing only for camber will not be a guarantee that your skis are the right flex. Here are four ways that can help you.

1. *You can give the skis the squeeze test.* Hold them, bottoms facing, and squeeze. Simple!—they should come together evenly the entire length, with the tips separating a little. Now grab another pair and squeeze them. If you test enough skis you will notice that some are softer than others.

   In general, if you have a ski the right length, you need a slightly softer (i.e., flexible) ski if you are light for your height, and a slightly stiffer ski if you are, shall I say, rugged for your height.

2. *You can use the paper-sliding test.* Put the skis on a smooth, hard floor; stand on them and have a friend try slipping a piece of paper under them where your feet are. If the paper slides between the floor and the skis comfortably, these skis are right for you. If the paper doesn't slide under, the skis are too soft. If there is a big gap and you could slide several pieces of paper underneath (or a piece of cardboard), the skis are too stiff.

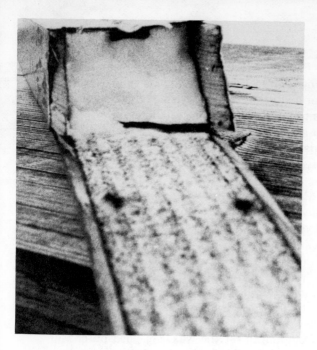

**7.** *This is not a marshmallow, but the light innards of a broken racing ski. These skis are too fragile for rough terrain.*

Many racers put marks on the sides of their skis to show how far the paper has slid fore and aft. This area is called the kicker zone, and is used as a guide in applying purchase waxes (which are discussed in Chapter 7, Waxing).

3. *Check the bottoms of waxable skis after a trial tour.* If the wax is worn evenly, the skis are the right flex for you. If the wax is worn off the tips and tails, the skis are too stiff. If the wax is worn off under the foot, the skis are too soft, or limber.

With waxless skis you can check them as you ski. If you get pretty good purchase on the flats and fairly good purchase on the uphills you certainly have some skis that are working. If the skis do slip it might be because of the conditions, so don't despair. Take the skis out another day, in different snow conditions, and see if they work better.

4. *Get a pair of skis from a company that indicates the flex on them.* For instance, I just got a pair that had a mark on a scale indicating the skis were suited for 65–75. One of my good friends asked me if that was an age category and I had to tell him it was for my weight, in kilograms.

Of the extremes, it's better to have a ski that is too limber. At least this way you can use the wax under the foot—where it's very important—until it wears off. Or, the waxless section of your ski—which is located primarily under the foot—will grab for you.

## Ski Widths

Most x-c skis are wider at tip and tail than at the waist. If you want to be exact and measure x-c skis for width at their tips and tails as well as right under the waist at the binding point, you will come up with at least a hundred different combinations. For purposes of simplification I group skis in three different categories, according to the width under the binding at the narrowest part of the ski. Touring skis are about 55 millimeters (2 1/16 inches) wide; light touring skis, about 48–51 mm (just less than 2 inches); racing skis, about 44–46 mm (well under 2 inches). Each ski has its special advantages.

But as I indicated at the outset, more and more tourskiers are using racing skis these days. With more and more touring centers around the country, tracks are more readily available and these are the skis for good tracks. Mine weigh less than 3 pounds, and some carbonfiber skis weigh less than 1,000 grams (about 2 pounds). These skis are designed specifically for skiing on well-prepared tracks, and if you try them and have difficulties turning them (having little, none, or reverse side camber, as mentioned below), or if you sink deep into unbroken snow, you have no one to blame but yourself.

Racing skis have undergone more radical changes in design than any others. For a while some racing skis had no side camber—that is, unlike the various tourers, their width measurements were the same at the tip, the waist and the tail. This made the racing skis difficult to turn, but the theory was that the tracks were so well set that the racers wouldn't need the conventional design. This wasn't enough so the manufacturers started making the boat-shaped models, with the tips narrower than the midsection. Faster, you know. At about the same time, though, the race courses became more challenging, often having what I call screaming, or fast, downhill sections with turns. Many racers couldn't hang on to these turns, partly because of their skis, which did not turn easily. At this writing, most knowledgeable racers choose skis they can manage and take a bye on any particular sidecut design.

*Summarizing:* The wider the ski is, the more it weighs. Fiberglass skis are usually lighter and more rugged than their wood counterparts. Racing skis are usually much lighter, more fragile, and harder to turn than touring or light touring skis.

You should thoroughly investigate your possibilities for skiing and then get the appropriate pair of skis. For instance, it's no good to buy wide touring skis if you plan to ski a lot with people who are using racing skis in good tracks. You'll be playing catch-up all day. On the other hand, those sleek racing skis will bog you down if you're going out touring with a group equipped for some deep snow skiing.

## THE POLES

The lightest, and most expensive, poles being made these days are used for racing. They utilize carbonfiber construction, weigh about 120 grams, or about five ounces, and cost around $85.00.

You can get poles made of fiberglass, metal or tonkin (bamboo). It's worth your time to get metal or fiberglass because they will not break so easily as tonkin.

### General Checklist

There are some things to watch for in choosing an all-purpose x-c pole:

1. *Get your poles the right height.* Stand on the floor, and the poles should fit comfortably under your armpits. Unless you're a kid. Then the poles can be shorter.
2. *It should go without saying now, but be sure the pole tip is curved* so that it pulls out of the snow when you ski. Don't get stuck with a straight-tipped Alpine pole, which will hang up in the snow as your ski slides by it.
3. *Look to see if the straps are rigged differently* so as to provide for a right pole and a left pole, and if the straps are adjustable. The part of the strap that comes out of the handle on top of the other part should be on the outside as you pole. If the straps are adjustable you can essentially vary your pole length according to snow conditions, or according to who is using the poles.

**8.** *Three pole baskets, the one on the left being for deep snow. The other two are racing versions for packed snow.*

# BOOTS AND BINDINGS

It's difficult for me to believe that manufacturing companies have us customers in mind when they keep coming out with new boot-binding combinations. No sooner do we get settled in with a decent system than the model changes, or some company offers something brand new which our dealer switches over to—and we are left out in the cold.

I've thought a lot about this problem and now suggest the following: After finding a pair of boots and bindings that suit you, get another set. You might even get a bargain at the end of a season. And you might get a spare binding or two, to use on an extra pair of skis or for parts in case one breaks. Then you will be set for a long time and can watch your friends frantically switching models or systems, and paying dearly for it, during the next few seasons.

You can be sure there are still designers out there trying to build better mousetraps and better boot-binding combinations. (It's interesting to note that one of the early, best-known Norwegian bindings is named Rottefella, translated rat-trap.) So we will surely see at least one new system every time we have an Olympics or World Championships event in cross-country—and these come along three years of every four now!

One wag suggested that a company was working on a computerized system which would tell you the wax for the day. Lately, I've learned not to scoff at such ideas.

Boot and binding compatibility is so important that these two equipment items are treated together. If you are getting equipment, the first rule is to make sure your boots fit the bindings.

There have been more different bindings on the market in the last 40 years than I would care to recount. Just a few years back some silly people thought everything was settled when most of the major ski equipment manufacturers agreed on the Nordic Norm. This was simply a standard sizing for all boots and bindings that were to be produced; this to insure compatibility. Then you could fit Norwegian boots to Finnish bindings, and so on.

The Nordic Norm sizing is still a going thing and the sizes are 71 mm, 75 mm and 79 mm. These distances are approximately the widths of the boots and bindings measured across the binding pins. In addition, the shapes of the bindings and boot sole are determined so that all left boots fit the appropriate left bindings, etc.

That made things too easy because the racing crowd, spurred by the Adidas Company, came up with a brand new boot and binding combination. Their boot has a snout, or toe piece, extending forward from a point where the conventional boot sole used to end. This snout is 38 mm wide and now this boot-binding combination is sometimes referred to as the Racing 38.

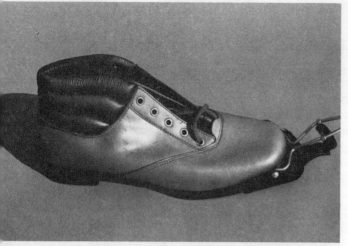

**9.** *A light touring boot in a three-pin binding.*

**10.** *The Adidas racing boot/binding combination.*

**11.** *The Salomon racing boot/binding combination.*

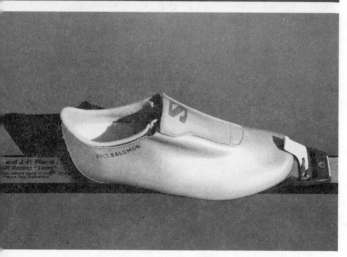

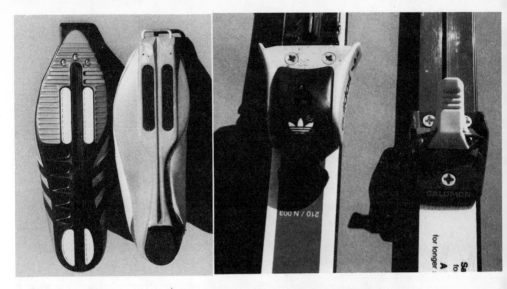

**12. and 13.** *The grooves in the soles of the Adidas (r) and the Salomon (l) boots are seen clearly. They mate with the ridges on the bindings in 13.*

There are two advantages to racers using Norm 38 rather than the Nordic Norm. The boot snout gives a skier more freedom or flexibility when striding. In short, he can take longer strides. Second, the bindings, being so narrow, do not dig into or rub so much on the edge of the track and this in turn means slightly more speed.

Most of the Nordic Norm group answered with their own, similar, boot-binding combination and this is now known as the Norm 50 because the boot snout and the bindings measure approximately 50 mm at the point where the binding pins fit into the boots.

So far, so good?

Many tourskiers began using either the Norm 38 or the Norm 50 but one of the complaints that came back was that the boots were too cold. While racers can generate a fair amount of heat and keep their feet warm, it didn't always work that way with the touring crowd.

The new boots had soles that were 7 mm thick and the manufacturers decided to make a touring model with a thicker sole, 12 mm, to be exact. So we now have the 50/7 Racing boot, or Norm, and the 50/12.

This was a fairly good idea and the only problem was that some of the thicker soled boots didn't fit the bindings which were designed for the thinner soles. Back to the drawing board! Sure enough, they fixed that so the bindings fit both boots and everyone was happy.

Not to be outdone, the Salomon Company came out with an entirely new combination called the Salomon Nordic System, or SNS. This system is not compatible with any others but Salomon has arrangements with some boot companies and they use the SNS boot fixture and then their boot fits a Salomon binding. SNS is gaining popularity rapidly.

19

14. *A Salomon bootie covering a boot.*

You may think we have seen the final word but I know some podiatrists and physicists have plans for us. You see, we have been using very inefficient boot-binding combinations all these years and that should be corrected!

## The Fit

Fit is the most important consideration in any boot you get. I like my boots to feel comfortable when I'm wearing two pair of socks. Boots that are too tight will cut down on blood circulation and cause cold feet. Boots that are too loose may allow extra movement and blister build-up.

## Materials

Some boots are advertised as having thermal soles, or thermal uppers. Find out what the manufacturer means by this. If the boots are indeed warmer than others, give you good support, and breathe, then you've got a good combination.

Don't reach blindly for a boot that may be waterproof, from outside, only to discover it doesn't breathe and that your feet sweat so much you end up each tour with wet feet anyway.

The ideal materials for boots are those which provide good support, keep your feet warm, resist water penetration, and breathe. Naturally, this is a tall order and there may have to be a few trade-offs. You'll be happiest researching your own feet's characteristics and then getting the boots that are best suited for you.

## Heel Set-Ups

We used to be happy with a piece of linoleum, or stair tread, under our heels to prevent snow build-up. Recently, most boot manufacturers have designed their boot soles to match plates on the ski to give you better lateral stability when your foot is flat on the ski, as in turning, or in doing a skating maneuver. This advance is a good one, but even then my boot twists off the ski in certain situations.

# Caring for Equipment

I've always been kind of a nut about maintenance. Whether it's new skis, a lawnmower, a car, or whatever, I set out to try to make the darned things last. It's easy to form a mystical association with a car through long years of use—many of us have done this. And I know plenty of people who get attached to particular skis, or boots or poles or bindings during the lifetime of such equipment. All of them have learned the best ways to care for the stuff and try to get the most use from it. Seldom do these skiers have equipment problems and, more important to many of us, this kind of long-range approach is the most economical.

There is enough information here to serve you and your equipment well. If you take some time to work on your skis especially you'll be rewarded with better performance on the snow.

## CARING FOR YOUR SKIS

Let's look at the skis in three different situations: first, when they're new; next, during the season as you are using them; and, finally, when you store them for the summer.

### Conditioning New Skis

#### IF THEY'RE FIBERGLASS

New fiberglass skis come with essentially two different kinds of bottoms. One is harder than the other but both are referred to often as "P-tex," or polyethylene. (I hesitate even to mention these terms since many firms have their own special-sounding, self-promoting, modern chemical-like brand names, and they like to differentiate between all the various formulas as if they were addressing the American Chemical Society, or some such group.)

FOR THE SOFTER BOTTOMS

Most new skis need sanding before you wax them. Get a block and a couple of different grades of sandpaper and smooth the bottoms and grooves. Begin with the coarser paper and finish with the smoother, naturally. One suggested sequence is to begin with 100 grit then move on to 150 and finish up with 180–220. Fussy people use finer paper for colder, drier snow.

After this, the bottoms should be hot-waxed—sometimes referred to as base-waxed—before using. The best way to do this is by ironing in some Alpine soft wax (for wet snow; see the Waxing chapter for this and other terms used below). This softer wax does a better job of combining with the bottom surface than a harder wax does.

Hold the Alpine wax against the tip of a hot ordinary flatiron close to the ski and draw a trail of wax on the bottom surface on each side of the groove. Then with the iron still on the setting at *Wool* (about 140° F/60° C), smooth the wax in. Spend some time going over the wax, since doing so insures a better job. In fact, if you hot-wax this base on several times during the season the performance of your skis will continue to improve.

After hot-waxing, scrape most of the wax off the bottom and the groove, leaving only a thin film. Metal or plastic scrapers may be used for this job, but if you use metal be sure not to scrape too hard or else you will take off some of the bottom surface as well as the wax.

Do not put Alpine wax on the area of the ski under the foot, where you will be applying x-c purchase (climbing) wax. Instead, use a hard x-c wax like Special Green, or a binder.

FOR HARDER BOTTOMS

Companies disagree on the preparation for fiberglass skis with the harder bottoms. Some will tell you not to worry, just go skiing. However, no harm is done by some light sanding and hot-waxing, as described above.

## If They're Wood

Wood skis almost became extinct during the late '70s and I thought I was going to be able to offer mine to museums as artifacts. But some companies still persist in making wood skis and it's good to see them, if only for the sake of tradition.

I was officiating at the NorAm X-C Races in January, 1984, and watched with amazement as Anne McKinnon skiied across the finish line in one race. She was competing on her wooden skis! She gave away a fair amount of time to the other competitors who all had fiberglass skis but she wasn't concerned with that. I thought it was a nice touch.

Most new wooden skis are sold with a coating of protective varnish

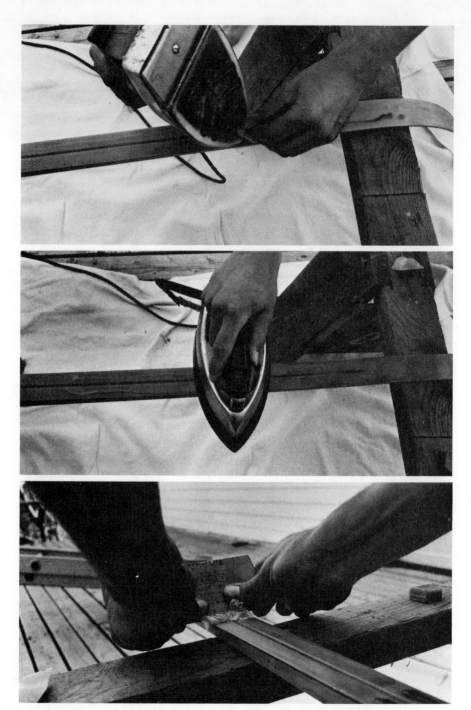

**15–17.** *Hot-waxing a fiberglass ski. Top (15) starting to "draw the bead" of speed wax from tip to tail, using a flatiron to melt it. In 16 (middle), smoothing the wax with a heat setting right for Wool. And at the bottom (17), scraping the wax to a thin film for optimum performance. Many waxers prefer using a plastic scraper for this job.*

or lacquer on the bottoms. This has to come off because it is deathly slow as a substitute for wax, and it doesn't even hold the wax you try to cover it with. I use a combination of strong liquid paint-remover and elbow grease—the elbow grease being needed to wield a scraper.

The most popular scraper with us is a flat rectangular steel one made by the Stanley tool company. This really has eight edges—each side of the rectangle counts as one, and you can flip it over for four more—which can be sharpened with a file when they get dull. There are lots of scrapers made especially for skis, many of which have rounded sections that are good for scraping the groove. If you don't have a tool for the groove you can round off a corner of the rectangular scraper. Or try a sharpened nail-head, holding it with a pair of pliers; or a sharpened screw-head. We've even shaped and sharpened narrow steel spoons and used them to clean out the groove. Having a groove tool will be helpful in scraping wax off your skis, too.

After scraping, the bottoms should be sanded smooth. Then if you want the ultimate in smoothness, polish the bottoms with steel wool.

Now they are ready for pine-tarring.

---

**HEATING A SKI**

Whenever you use heat on any ski bottom you run the risk of damaging the ski. With the old wood skis many a person used to burn the bottoms when applying pine tar with a torch. Well, there's no need to pine-tar the plastic bottoms, but you still can melt the plastic by using too much heat. If you have had a lot of experience with these new ski bottoms you may have done this already. If you vigorously sand or wire-brush the damaged section there is a good chance you can get rid of the scar tissue and the bottom will be ready for hot-waxing again.

Sometimes it's necessary to use a lot of heat either to apply wax or to clean it off your skis. I've already dealt with the danger of overheating a fiberglass bottom and will just add this for now: Synthetic skis hold heat very well, and you should give them a long time to cool outside before using. Occasionally heat will put some extra camber in wood skis (though the extra bend doesn't last long). If you are satisfied with the camber in your skis and have just finished using a lot of heat on the bottoms, turn the skis over and heat the tops. This should keep things in balance. But be careful not to burn the finish.

In using a torch of any sort great care should be exercised. I've seen so many skis singed, even charred, by skiers who weren't paying attention. The situation with non-wood bottoms can be worse. Some of these don't singe or turn black like wood; instead, they start burning! A hole in a synthetic bottom isn't easy to repair.

There are at least two reasons for using tar, or some similar substance. First, the pine tar helps seal the bottom. Next, it also helps to hold the x-c wax you apply on top of it (and pine tar isn't the worst stuff in the world to ski on all by itself). I used to tar my wood skis for still another reason: I like the smell of it.

The tars used to come in instant spray-on, wipe-on and just plain old burn-it-in varieties. These are put out by some wax companies but since most skis are fiberglass now, and since you don't use pine tar on these new models, pine tar is sometimes hard to come by. Go to your hardware store if you have trouble finding it in a ski shop.

To burn it in apply some to the ski bottoms and heat gently with a torch until it bubbles a bit. Wipe it to spread it around some more and heat again. If you're a fanatic you can go on for hours doing this. We used to when we thought the whole process had a great deal of mystique attached to it. I'm not sure the pine tar penetrated the wood much farther. After "burning the tar in," you can leave the skis overnight in a warm room but before you apply x-c wax you should wipe the bottoms until they are just a bit tacky. You may have to heat the bottom again to do this.

## During the Season

During the season your Alpine base-wax will wear off fiberglass skis, and the pine tar will wear off the wood ones. In both cases the bottom will have a whitish look, which you should take care of. Simply scrape the skis clean and apply the base-wax as before.

### FIBERGLASS

Or the bottoms of your fiberglass skis may become gouged and these holes should be filled. Clean out the holes by scraping and sanding, or wire-brushing, and then fill the depressions with a Kofix candle—a special soft plastic compound, carried by many ski shops—melted in, or some epoxy glue, or some other plastic specified by the manufacturer. After the filler hardens, sand it off so it is flush with the bottom surface and you're ready to go skiing again.

Waxless ski bottoms may need attention after a few outings even though they're not gouged. Fishscales, ridges, and diamonds can get clogged by these same impurities. The skis become less effective and should be cleaned. Wipe the ski bottoms with a solvent for wax or grease, to get them back to normal. Now you'll be all set.

### WOOD

Wood bottoms will also get rough. They get gouged by sharp objects; splinters are likely to appear; sometimes granular snow is tough on any bottom.

If you have plastic, lignostone or hickory edges, the bottom surface down the middle occasionally wears down, leaving the harder material in the edges protruding and producing what we call "railing." (When this happens you know either that your wax has not been holding well enough to protect the ski, or that you have been skiing in some very coarse snow conditions—which sometimes can't be avoided.) This railing effect is serious. The edges behave like runners and make the ski more difficult to turn or slide around—you'll think they are downhill skis, they go so straight. More important, when the ski does slide sideways there is an increased danger of hooking sharp objects in under the edge and tearing off a section of it. If this happens you're in real trouble, and the best thing to do is get a craftsman to cut out this section of your ski and put in a new little block of wood as a patch.

All these kinds of damage should be corrected by a thorough job of smoothing again. You can be fairly vigorous in scraping wood bottoms: You might get a cup or so of fine shavings. I've seen wood skis scraped so much that the groove is noticeably shallower.

If you're still left with a gouge or hole after this smoothing or scraping, then you should fill the spot with plastic wood.

SIDES AND TOPS OF WOOD SKIS

The sides of the ski should be kept clean. Most people don't scrape the finish off the sides; but after it begins to wear off anyway, it's wise to keep the sides waxed. Common paraffin, the stuff used for covering homemade jelly, is fine for this.

The tops get nicked, too, after a while. I never refinish the top, but you might want a different appearance. Again, it's a good idea to keep the tops waxed with paraffin. This serves two purposes: It keeps the snow from building up on your skis so you don't have to carry it along with you, and it helps protect the wood from moisture.


## Major In-season Repairs for Waxless Skis

FIBERGLASS DELAMINATION

Fiberglass skis may delaminate because of poor handling. Like jamming your ski tails down into the snow to prop them up while you take a break from skiing. Or from exposing the slight cracks in the lamination to alternating hot and cold conditions. If a small amount of water gets into a crack, then freezes, it usually expands the crack. Next time more water gets in, etc., and you've got trouble.

To repair such a ski, bring it in and dry it thoroughly. Then spread open the delaminated area without force, and clean it. Fill the separation with epoxy, being sure to push the glue in deep, then squeeze the layers together rather gently.

Here is a tricky situation when you can squeeze out all the glue if you try hard enough. But don't. Wrap waxed paper around the repaired area then clamp it, but not at full pressure: Wait an hour before you draw up the clamps to full. After the epoxy dries you should be able to remove the clamps easily from the ski because the waxed paper will have prevented them from sticking to the ski.

## FOR TRAVEL, A SKI BAG

The competitors who fly around the world have always packed their skis and poles in ski bags for ease of transporting. Now, ski bags are becoming popular everywhere for travel by car, bus or train, and I strongly recommend them. They are easy to attach to a car ski rack, hold lots of equipment, and protect the skis from all that junk that flies up off the road during winter travel.

They're easy to make. Get someone to sew up some tough denim or heavy sailcloth; leave one end open for packing, and allow for a fold-over closure or a zipper. Put a carrying handle (or reinforced strap of the material, of convenient length) lengthwise near the middle where the balance is best for you, and you're all set.

Or you can buy a bag.

## Storing Your Skis

After the snow season it's best to leave wax on all types of bottoms for summer storage.

One theory holds that a wood ski will better maintain its shape if the stresses resulting from heat and moisture are equal on the tops and bottoms. This is apparently why the skis are lacquered top and bottom at the factory. It wouldn't do to have a wood bottom untreated and exposed to different atmospheric conditions, while the top, because of its finish, remained unaffected. (You probably wouldn't leave one side of a door untreated, unless you wanted it to warp.) Anyway, this is my excuse for not cleaning the klister off my skis in the spring.

Fiberglass skis shouldn't warp on you, but it is important to treat them like new skis before storing. If you leave the bottoms without wax they will oxidize and then next season won't work so well when you go skiing. So, clean them up and iron in a good coat of that Alpine soft wax you used as a conditioner. And this time I wouldn't scrape off any excess. Just leave all of it on for the summer.

I try to store my skis in a cool, dry place, where the temperature won't change radically all the time.

And I do *not* block any of them together. The best reason for not blocking them together and trying to put more camber in them is this, as it was once explained to me: If you can block the skis and put more camber in them, it will be a simple matter to take it out by skiing on them. So blocking won't do any good.

## Caring for Ski Bindings

FIRST, MOUNT THEM RIGHT

Bindings should be mounted so that the toe of the boot is approximately over the balance point of the ski. If your shop has not mounted them for you, use the directions that come with the bindings themselves.

With wood skis, mounting bindings is a routine operation; anyone with the right-sized drills and a screwdriver can do the job. But with the fiberglass construction prevalent nowadays a more complicated procedure is usually necessary.

You should know this so you don't come a cropper like the fellow on the Swedish relay team in the 1974 FIS Championships. He had just received a new pair of fiberglass skis—that was the year of the fiberglass breakthrough—and put the bindings on in the usual manner; that is, he drilled holes and screwed the bindings on. The trouble was, though, the inside of the ski was mostly foam. You know, it's lighter, and all that. Well, he led off for the relay, sprinted part of the way out of the start, and popped out of one binding. The meet was in Sweden and all the TV cameras were glued on him as he ran around, looking rather embarrassed, and found a replacement ski. Later on he popped out of the other ski, got a replacement, and was eventually disqualified for taking on *two* new skis.

Since then the companies have been making the skis' innards out of more substantial material, particularly under the foot where there is so much stress and where you are going to drill holes. The procedure for mounting bindings is simple enough. *But first this warning:* Some glues like epoxy react with the material inside certain fiberglass skis and eat it away, so you should check with your ski shop or supplier to make sure you're choosing a glue that will work right for your particular make of ski.

O.K. Drill the holes for the screws, fill them with the correct glue, mount the bindings—and then turn the skis over so they are bottoms up while the glue sets. This way the glue will pool around the binding screws and harden there—instead of leaking out into an air channel in the inside of the ski, or getting otherwise dispersed.

It's a good idea to lubricate screws with ordinary Vaseline or silicone before putting them into any ski: this makes them easier to take out if a situation ever requires it. However, if the screws are epoxied in, you may have to use heat to loosen them.

IF THE MOUNTINGS LOOSEN

Problems occur when the binding screws loosen. The binding wiggles and the screw holes enlarge. (Have you ever been out on a long tour and lost a binding? Good luck!)

If the holes get much too large, stuff them with a wooden matchstick or a wood golf tee and some glue, and re-drill. Or plug the holes completely, and move the binding slightly forward or backward to a new location for fresh screw holes. If the screws come loose just occasionally, plug them with a little steel wool and some matchsticks, then put the screws back in.

Of course, by keeping the screws tight all the time you can avoid the trouble of such repairs.

### IF THE BOOTS LOOSEN

If the pin holes in the boot sole get too large, you can fill them with epoxy glue and re-drill.

Another problem arises when the boot shrinks slightly and does not fit snugly in the binding. Then the boot wiggles and, if you have a pin-binding, the holes in the boot are likely to get too large. So check the binding fit carefully. If the boot has shrunk, try hammering in the sides of the binding, or adjusting it if you can. On some bindings this can't be done.

In every case, try to keep a tight fit between the boot and the side of the binding.

*Note:* You can actually wax your bindings to keep the snow off. There are also some de-icing compounds which keep ice from forming on the bindings and at the same time keep the moving parts loose.

## Caring for Boots and Poles

### SKI BOOTS

There isn't much difference between caring for x-c boots and caring for shoes, or other kinds of boots. I use either wax polish or a waterproofing material such as silicone on the leather part of the boot.

If the boots get wet, *dry them slowly.* Some leather boots will crack if you bring them in wet and dry them rapidly on the top of a radiator or heat duct. To help in drying you can fill the insides with wadded newspaper or other absorbent material.

Check your boot laces occasionally and replace them if they are worn. No sense fumbling with cold hands out on the trail trying to tie together the ends of busted laces.

### SKI POLES

Two situations can really embarrass you.

One is having the handle strap tear or break. You should be able to notice any weak spots in the strap and tape them, or replace the entire strap. I know straps don't tear very often, but if it ever happens to you I think you'll be amazed to find out how much you depend on them.

The other situation is more common, and it's a killer. You guessed it—the basket falls off in the middle of a tour. If you haven't tried skiing in deep snow with a basketless pole you haven't met with one of the ultimates in frustration. So, better check the cotterpin, wire, glue, or whatever holds your basket on. It's safer to repair the system once a year than suffer on the trail.

You ought to use paraffin wax or de-icer on your pole baskets too. If the basket has wood or leather products in it, waxing also protects them from moisture. More important, wax helps keep the snow off the basket and makes lifting the pole easier.

---

### REPAIRING A BROKEN WOOD SKI

More skiers mean more broken skis, but if we go the route of all-fiberglass unbreakable skis, there won't be this problem. In the meantime, many repairmen are having good luck making a "new" ski from the broken pieces of a wooden ski by using liquid fiberglass. Douse the broken ends of the pieces with fiberglass, stick them together, and then put them in a mold.

The best do-it-yourself mold you can get, especially for a ski-tip job, is to use two sound skis that are the same shape your broken one used to be. Take the bindings off two skis, wrap the good skis with waxed paper around the area of repair (so they won't get gunk on them); nestle the three skis spoon-fashion, putting one good ski with the binding on top and one on the bottom of the broken ski—which is by this time freshly repaired with the fiberglass—and clamp everything together overnight to let the fiberglass harden in place.

The next day you can take the skis apart, sand the repaired one, put the bindings back on, and go skiing.

# 3

# What to Wear

Back in the 1950's when x-c was fairly rare it was easy to identify the serious x-c'er. He almost always wore baggy knickers and carried around with him those long tonkin poles with the big baskets. Some fashion people got hold of the knickers idea (yes, even then) and promoted them for general wear by all skiers. I raced the old Wildcat downhill trail in New Hampshire in 1952 wearing knickers. Slow time, too.

About the time x-c started its first boom, during the '60s, knickers weren't so special any more, at least with the tourskiers. Whether they wanted to appear special, or whether they wanted to wear any darned thing that suited them, I don't know. But the tourskiers just showed on the scene in any kind of get-up that occurred to them. Old army gear was a favorite.

The developments in new clothing and the science of dressing properly have been overshadowed by reports of progress in ski design, new waxes and boots, and all those sort of things. Maybe the clothing people need new marketing management because I think the changes in clothing that have occurred recently are the most significant benefits for the skier. The clothing market has opened up in North America and it's safe to say that manufacturers are producing so many different styles and types that we are the world leaders in the variety of clothes for x-c. The traditionalist may not cotton to the new designs—which include wild colors and one-piece suits—but they're here to stay. So, as with equipment, if you look around long enough you will probably be able to find anything that fits your needs.

*Note:* There is more about clothing in Kid Stuff, Chapter 6.

## Basics to Keep in Mind

Before I itemize today's clothing choices there are a few general points that should be made.

Be sure to follow the layering principle. Many light layers of appropriate materials are better than one or two layers of anything.

The layering principle has the following important advantages: It allows you flexibility. When you get too warm you can shed a garment and wrap it around your waist or stuff it in your pack. The layers also trap air between them and it's the air that provides you with good insulation against the cold. Two layers of air are better than one, and so on. Finally, if the clothing is of the right material it will help keep you warm by wicking perspiration, insulating you, and protecting you from wind and moisture in the form of rain or snow.

From the inside out, you should wear polypropylene underwear, or some similar material. This has a high wicking ability and will carry your perspiration away from your skin, thus preventing it from evaporating and cooling on your skin. You can still wear your baggies, old uniforms, dungarees, or whatever over your underwear and no one will ever know. But shy away from all nylon or something that won't breathe or else you're apt to be bathed in puddles of perspiration.

This polypro stuff is the greatest advance in clothing I've seen. It really saves a lot of chills and probably colds as well. But it needs constant washing and after a while it kind of decomposes. Don't be caught wearing unwashed polypropylene at big social occasions in crowded, warm rooms.

Your next layer should be one that provides insulation. Wool may be the best because it retains insulative qualities even when wet, but other materials such as polyester, nylon, acrylic, and olefin are good. The outside layer should be wind and water resistant. Nylon, polyester, and tightly woven wool are all good. New materials such as Gore-Tex, which breathe, yet are nearly waterproof, are also good.

Try to adjust your exercise level or activity to the clothing you are wearing *and* try to adjust your clothing to the exercise level or activity you are pursuing.

For instance, if you start out on a day's tour with three or four layers on your upper body, shed one or two, or even three, if it is necessary to keep from sweating a lot. If you are in this state of "undress" and come to a long, downhill slope, throw on at least a windbreaker for the trip down.

If you are caught out on a short tour feeling cold and wearing all the clothes you have for the trip, speed up a bit and warm yourself this way.

Now we come to some trade-offs.

The new one-piece x-c suits are warmer than two-piece suits of the same material but it's hard to wriggle in and out of these when you want to cool off or answer the calls of nature.

The tight-fitting stretch garments look flashy, but the fact that they stretch indicates that the weave is not so tight and therefore not so wind resistant, unless your suit has an extra layer sewn inside the front, top to bottom. This helps guard against windchill.

In some instances it will be your previous experience or conditioning that carries you through a long trip because it can be difficult, or awkward at least, to be wearing the proper clothing for every little change in condition. When I skied the 1979 Norwegian Birkebeiner I was equipped with Lifa polypropylene underwear and a special Lifa Birkebeiner model racing suit with windpanels in the front. It was a Special Green wax day with temperatures during my five-hour jaunt ranging from $-10$ to $-15°$ C, yet I was warm enough with only those two layers, partly because I was hurrying along and generating a little heat of my own. In fact, at times I skied long stretches without gloves, just like the Russians. My head sweat a lot (see below) and I did switch hats. The 5 kg pack, required of all my racers, helped keep me warm, too.

Had I been out for a tour in weather like this I most certainly would have worn, or carried along, an extra layer of clothing. For coaching in weather like this I would have a set of warm-ups on top of everything. But that's my preference. You will be in different situations and will have to experiment a bit before finding the optimum dress.

## Knickers, Pants, or One-Piece Suits

The racers introduced one-piece suits and they are very popular now, even with tourskiers. They come in two basic styles: full length, which

18. *A motley array of outfits with the only common apparel being gloves.*

**19.** *Racing suits are just about the lightest thing you can wear for skiing. Here two coaches in warm-up suits run alongside their racers giving them splits.*

have a strap under the foot (and with which you wear short socks) and below-the-knee length, which require the traditional knicker socks.

The full length suit has just about taken over this market and now most skiers will be wearing it, or the more traditional knickers and separate tops.

Knickers are the traditional x-c pants and come in various materials. I would get light ones that are wind and water resistant and be prepared to wear an extra layer or two underneath in the event of cold weather. An old pair of long underwear, cut off around the knees, makes a good undergarment. The new polypropylene underwear is very tight fitting and can be easily worn full length.

Warm-up pants are increasingly popular. These were brought in by the racing crowd and were used primarily to warm up in before a race, and to stay warm in after a race. Immediately before a race they were shed in favor of a racing suit. Now, since warm-ups feel so good, lots of skiers use them instead of suits. If they are fairly snug around the lower leg they don't allow any scuffing. And, if you're going to stand around a lot, as coaches do, they're better than suits or knickers, being warmer. Wear 'em myself.

These are traditional items, remember. But—while I wouldn't go so far as to recommend bell bottoms—lots of other combinations are possible. If it's warm, shorts are just great. Or you can try the "Putney springtime uniform"—long underwear with shorts on top. It's very fast on the downhills because there is so little wind resistance. (I haven't seen many x-c'ers in leotards, but they would be fastest of all!)

## Hats and Earbands

It's been estimated the body loses 25 percent of its heat through the head. When I ski, I like a hat or an earband, or both, to soak up some of the sweat, because the more sweat I can keep out of my eyes, the better. At the same time it's important to have material in your headgear that will breathe. You've probably seen skiers come in after a long workout, their hats covered with hoarfrost. This has come from their little old heads, and has just frozen on there.

On real warm days you might not need a hat. If it's mildly cold, you might get away with an earband. If it's very cold, you might want both an earband and a hat. This is a very good combination for bitter weather.

Don't be afraid to overdress in the hat division. There isn't any problem to tucking an extra earband or hat into your pocket, and it might come in very handy for a long downhill run following a warm climb.

## Gloves

Well, my favorite gloves are still those cotton work jobbies affectionately known in English racing circles as "French-Canadian racing gloves." Since writing the first edition, the price of these beauties has risen from 39 cents, but I still find them the best buy on the market. You can go whole hog and get real, ventilated, racing gloves for around $25.00 at this writing, and there are lots of in-betweens. Some racers have used handball gloves. These also breathe: they're full of holes!

There are lots of mittens addicts. I happen to prefer gloves because they allow a much more sensitive feel for the poling action. However, there's no question that mittens are warmer.

In very cold weather some skiers Vaseline their hands, or rub on some talcum powder; I'm not sure either helps. Another trick is to wear a pair of silk gloves as liners under another pair of gloves or mittens.

If you're desperate for lack of gloves or mittens some day, pull a pair of socks on over your hands. They're better than nothing at all.

## Socks

If you have knickers you're sort of bound to use knicker socks. If you don't, you'll get mighty cold. Wool socks are the best since they are warm and shed moisture very well. There are other lighter, tighter-fitting socks and you pay the price for this lightness. You don't stay as warm, but if that's not a problem, O.K.

The skiers in the full length suits wear sock combinations that vary according to taste but provide a comfortable fit with the boot. Wearing too many socks and cramping your feet will cut down blood circulation and result in cold feet.

If you're wearing long pants and don't need knicker socks, you should try the so-called thermal socks. I've had good luck with them.

I've seen some skiers wrap a plastic freezer bag over their socks before the boot goes on. If they're going out in real wet weather, or know they're going to get wet feet, they claim this helps.

## Avoiding Cold, Wet Feet

It's easy to get wet feet, and this is the complaint I hear most about. Skiers' feet can even sweat enough to get socks and boots wet, to say nothing of the snow and other elements working on your feet from the outside. There are a few steps you can take to help avoid this problem.

1. *Gaiters,* which are becoming very popular. These fit over the top of your boot at the ankle. The biggest job they do, I think, is to keep the snow from going down inside your boot; snow seeping in here is the surest way to get wet feet. So, if you're going to be skiing in deep snow a lot, you should invest in a pair of gaiters. They come in many sizes, from very narrow on up to knee length.
2. *Boot-gloves made of rubberized material will keep your boots dry from the outside although you may still sweat from the inside and eventually get wet feet anyway.* Boot-gloves made of other materials are generally meant to keep your feet warm and I find these more useful in our area. If you can't find boot-gloves, or don't want to pay the price for them, cut the toes off an old pair of socks and pull them right on over your boots.
3. *Polish your boots regularly; or use waterproofing compounds.* Either will help to repel moisture from the outside—and it goes without saying that dry boots help to keep feet warm.
4. *Some new boots have materials like Gore-Tex in their uppers and these will allow foot perspiration to escape more easily.* So if you have sweaty feet, these boots may be the answer for you.
5. *For very cold weather lots of skiers swear by the silk socks-talcum powder routine.* They rub talcum powder on their feet,

pull on a pair of silk socks and then follow with their other socks. You can try it.

6. *Allow your boots to cool off when you step outside your door to go skiing.* Stand still a minute or two in the cold air before rushing right into the snow with warm boots; otherwise the snow will melt on your boots and you'll be on your way toward wet feet.

## After Skiing

The best thing to do after a tour is to dry off and keep warm. If you have a shower and a change of clothing available, that's fine. If you don't and you're stuck somewhere, there are a couple of things you can do.

I suppose the most welcome item after a workout is a dry turtleneck. If you can bring one of these along with you, jump right into it. You might even want to rub yourself off with snow first. It's very refreshing.

If you don't have any extra clothing to change into, try this. Switch the order of your shirts. Sometimes the outside shirt is the drier, and you can put that on right next to your skin. Put the wet one on the outside—and maybe it will dry soon, too.

## Goggles and Packs

Until recently, the use of goggles in x-c was always considered a No-No. The problem used to be that the goggles steamed up so much that you couldn't see through them.

But now they've improved the ventilation system enough on some models to make fogging no longer a problem. And a few skiers are using them. Better yet, if you can get hold of a Con Shield from West Yellowstone, Montana, it will protect your eyes from the cold and the snow. Some skiers, particularly racers, injure their eyes when they ski in a snowstorm or in very cold weather. Recently, a skier who was leading in a National Championship race had to withdraw because his eyes froze up on a long downhill. A layer of ice over his eyes impaired his vision—understatement of the day.

At the Sarajevo 1984 Olympics the Russian Zimjatov borrowed a Con Shield from an American and went on to win the gold medal in the men's 30 km event. It was snowing heavily at the time.

If the sun is very bright and you're going to be out a long time, you could wear goggles with dark lenses to protect your eyes. Sunglasses are better, however, and I would recommend them, especially in the spring when the sun gets higher and brighter. You also might invest in one of those elastic bands that go around the back of the head to keep the glasses from slipping off when you're really moving.

A good item to have is a fannypack that straps around your waist. Also called a kidney pack, it is a shaped pouch that straps around your waist and is worn out of the way below the small of your back. You can put extra wax, corks, snacks, socks, etc., in one of these and carry it along with ease on your outings. They come in several sizes.

# 4

# Technique

THE MOST FUN IN x-c skiing is moving around the terrain any way you like, and personal enjoyment should be your most important consideration. However, I feel there are many skiers who like to work on their technique and this chapter is written for them. I am describing the classic form here because I think it is the best way to ski.

If you are a family skier and want to work at it, I'm sure you can learn to go fast over certain sections of the track and get that thrill of speed which comes easily with the proper technique. If you're a racer you should read the more specialized approach in my other book on training and technique.*

*But if you want to do your own thing and ski your own way, just skip this chapter* and no one will be the loser. I'm serious about this.


## A DIFFERENT APPROACH—AND WHY

In this edition I'm going to describe my favorite way of teaching beginning skiers.

This system starts out by emphasizing certain arm movements. Hey, wait a minute! you say—the *legs* are the most important part of the body in skiing!

I agree. So I'll say it, too. The legs are the most important limbs in

---

*Caldwell on Competitive Cross-Country Skiing. *The Stephen Greene Press,* 1979.

skiing x-c, and provide by far the most strength, power and stability. I merely emphasize use of the arms in this method because I think it's a good way to learn. For the following reasons:

1. *In beginning to learn a skill sport, most North Americans are far more adept with their arms than they are with their legs.*

   You recall the old trick of testing arm vs leg coordination by throwing a ball to someone: If he catches it with his hands, he's from North America; if he traps it with his feet he's from Europe. The difference occurs because of North Americans' ingrained preference for such games as baseball, basketball and our brand of football, as compared with the Europeans' being brought up on soccer, where touching the ball with your hands is illegal unless you're the goalie.

   Thus I find that North Americans generally have good control of their hand and arm movements—which makes it quite easy to teach them basic x-c skiing movements by starting with emphasis on the arms.

2. *Despite good control of arm movements, many Americans have weak arms and shoulders, measured in cross-country terms.* All the learning steps that I suggest can also be used as drills to build strength and coordination in your upper body.

3. *This system is probably unique.* Which makes it fresh. And fun.

   You can read about the traditional methods that stress leg movements in my earlier books, or in other people's books for that matter; there are also lots of professional ski-touring groups in the United States and the Dominion which have good methods for teaching. All the ones I know of put prime emphasis on the legs, and start you off with a walking or shuffling motion.

   So there's no dearth of information on x-c technique, and I don't really want to argue the merits of various teaching systems. I have already written about the traditional methods. I thought I'd simply offer another approach this time around.

4. *And finally, the important thing is to be able to teach something—not the method that's used to teach it.*

   I guess my bag is education, and if there's one thing I've learned after several years in the field is that you can teach a thing in any number of ways. My approach, therefore, is offered not as an end-all, but rather as a way that might work well with a lot of skiers who are new to x-c, or who are teaching their friends or families.

## ON THE FLAT

### What You'll Arrive At: The Diagonal Stride

A well-executed diagonal stride is the hallmark of a practiced x-c'er. You've seen pictures of a good skier in full flight: Right arm reaching out ahead to set the pole, matched by the forward-driving left leg; left arm and right leg extending backward, almost parallel. If you drew lines from arm to arm and from leg to leg you'd see why we call this x-c signature "the diagonal."

Although the stride is a natural elongation of walking, if you're like me and try too consciously to correlate these movements, you may get all mixed up. But if you master the steps—meaning the stages—described below, you'll be well on your way. Thereafter it's only a matter of lots of practice. And your work will be repaid, for a good diagonal combines power (provided by the thrust of legs and poling action) with moments of relaxation as the limbs swing forward once more.

Technically speaking, nearly all phases of hill-climbing—as well as flat skiing—use the diagonal: that is, alternate legs and arms move in a coordinated fashion.

*Note:* This technique sometimes is referred to as the "single stride." I use the term myself but I can't explain its derivation: What would a double stride, or even a triple stride, be like? Probably rather difficult maneuvers . . .

There are four steps in the following sequence leading up to the diagonal, or single-stride, technique. The diagonal will remain the classic method of traveling on x-c skis for a long time to come. This is the stride that you will use in judging your own proficiency—or another skier's. This is the one you will most enjoy practicing, or skiing with, too.

### Step One: The Double-Pole

Are you ready to go? I will assume that your equipment is ready and your skis work—that is, they are waxed correctly or are waxless skis that work in the given conditions. I will also assume that you are skiing in tracks, packed out especially for x-c skiing.

The first exercise takes place on the flat or on a very gradual downhill. It's called double-poling, and you simply reach forward slightly and place both poles in the snow at enough of an angle so that, when you push down on them, the force will propel you forward along the tracks. Keep your elbows close to your body.

You may find you don't have enough strength to do this. If so, you'll have to train your arms gradually and build them up. Meanwhile, you

1

2

20–23. *A sequence showing the no-step double-pole.*

3

4

can try this exercise on a slightly steeper downgrade where you can coast without pushing on the poles. Begin coasting, then give a push with the poles to get the feel of it. After a few times you'll have the ability to go back to the flatter—i.e., less steep—downhill.

### TRY IT UPHILL

After your arms get stronger you can try double-poling on the flats—and then, believe it or not, *up* some gradual hills.

If you are a teaching purist you're going to get after me right now and ask how in the world this poor skier can get back up the hill if I haven't taught him how to walk or climb.

That's a good question and I'll answer it this way: This sequence is aimed primarily at teaching the single stride, or diagonal. I would hope that the teacher or the reader (pupil in this case) would get the whole sequence in mind before going out, and so perhaps would be able to apply the next steps to get back up the gradual hill.

I'll admit this will not work with some beginners. With them, there are two choices left. You let the beginner improvise. You might be surprised at what he will be able to do to get back up that little old hill.

Or you tell him to take off his skis and walk back to the beginning point.

## Step Two: Single-Poling

Here comes a really good builder of coordination and strength. In it you propel yourself along the track using just one arm at a time, alternately, while you keep your skis steady, like a sled's runners.

Place each pole at an angle so the force will propel you forward as you push down and back on it. In this poling motion you should begin to think about pushing each arm far enough to the rear so that your hand passes by your thigh. Don't worry about bending over with your upper body as you push down and back on the pole. Properly used, the upper body provides more force for this poling movement.

Again, it will be easier to start on a gentle downgrade. If you progress so you can do this on the flats, then on gradual uphills, you will have developed excellent strength and coordination, both of which will come in handy doing the diagonal stride. However, it's not necessary to be able to do this exercise uphill before proceeding to the next step.

## Step Three: One-Step Double-Pole

In this exercise you reach forward with both arms simultaneously, as in the double-pole, and at the same time, slide one ski forward. Then

**24–29.** *The no-step single pole. Strong arms are needed for this. Beginners should start on a slight downgrade.*

**1**

**3**

**5**

**30–34.** *A one-step double pole with the classic pose shown in picture 3 of this sequence.*

push down and back with the arms. Again, as in the single-poling drill, it will help to use your upper body to gain more power. If you keep your hands below your shoulders as you lean over in this maneuver chances are good that your form will be correct.

Practice so that you can slide either leg forward, and pole, using both arms forcefully. A good drill is to alternate your legs. Start with the left ski sliding ahead, pole, then coast a bit; slide the right leg ahead, double-pole, and coast. Continue.

At this point you may begin using your legs for some power. As you double-pole, give a little push, or bounce (here called a *kick*), off the leg you did not slide forward. If your skis aren't holding, or if you push too hard off this more stationary leg, your ski will slip back. If this happens, don't push back so hard with the rear leg. Instead, try pushing (kicking) *downward* more.

### REVIEW OF STEPS 1 THROUGH 3

A review is a good idea at this time. Make sure you can do the three preceding exercises fairly well. Pay attention to your armswing, so it is relaxed as it goes forward and there is enough extension beyond your hip as the arms push to the rear. I ask my skiers to continue pushing back with the arms, whether they are using them one or two at a time, so that I can see some daylight between their arms and hips.

## Step Four: The Diagonal Itself

To do the diagonal simply reach forward with your right arm and at the same time slide your left leg ahead; pole with your right arm and give a little push off your right leg. Then reach forward with your left arm, slide the right ski ahead and push with your left leg.

It's like walking. You alternate: right arm and left leg ahead, left arm and right leg behind.

If you've followed the sequence leading up to the diagonal, you haven't concentrated much on using your legs. But you ought to begin now. As you pole, give a slight push down and back with the more stationary leg—which has completed its glide and is ready to extend behind you— just as I suggested you do in the one-step double-pole.

When everything goes well you will glide a bit on the forward ski, then reach forward with the other arm and slide its opposite leg ahead simultaneously, pole, and push off the stationary leg, and soon you've got it. After a while you will gain some rhythm and will be able to slide along in near effortless fashion.

The more accomplished you get with the diagonal, the more likely you are to acquire a few individual stylistic flourishes that will keep

**35–40.** *The finished version: diagonal stride of a practiced skier.*

2

4

6

you from feeling too mechanical. Don't worry about them; they'll distinguish you from an automaton. For instance, I seem to cross one arm in front of my body, but not the other. And we had one skier on the U.S. Team who ran with his head cocked to one side.

The basic rule to follow in using the diagonal stride is this: *Try to make all your movements directly ahead.* Use economy of motion by making only those movements which contribute to carrying you straight along the track.

## A SUMMARY

The skier with the complete technique thinks about his forward movements as well as his kicking and poling efforts, which are primarily directed down and back. This is another reason I like to start beginners out with this sequence which emphasizes forward arm and leg movements.

I can describe the diagonal mainly in terms of the forward leg swing,

**41.** *Skiing without poles is good practice, especially if you try to stay in sync.*

like this: Imagine yourself perched on one ski that is fastened to the snow (this a result of setting your wax or gripping your surface). Now swing the other leg and ski forward, accelerating the speed. Naturally this is done with the aid of a downward kick on the stationary ski and a poling motion down and to the rear, but if you emphasize the forward leg movement and the forward motion of the arm which isn't helping to support you, you can begin to get the feeling of swinging down the track . . . almost reaching down the track. The forward arm swing can be combined with a slight opening of the angle at the waist (the angle between the upper body and the lower body) and this will in turn tend to unweight the forward part of the gliding ski and give a very slight planing effect. In addition, by changing the waistbend angle slightly it tends to relax you for an instant before you proceed with the next compression—which will take place on that forward leg, while the other one swings forward with acceleration.

I've had this feeling for about 5 percent of the times I've tried for it but it's so good that it's worth reporting to you. But don't worry unduly about it. It's an approach which should primarily concern the serious racers.

## HOW KICK OR PURCHASE AFFECTS YOUR TECHNIQUE

After a lot of study I've come up with the following conjecture: Too much purchase or kick wax can affect your technique adversely. I've noticed this particularly on the racing scene and you may want to take note of my observations, or simply disregard them. For how many of us are there who want to sacrifice even the smallest amount of kick just to take a chance on being able to ski "better"?

Here's what happens. Racers who frequently ask for bomb-proof kick on their skis—it can always be provided by waxing—begin to sit back a bit on their skis. The kicking motion becomes more drawn out, almost sluggish. The wax really holds and if they are a bit sloppy setting their wax due to not riding a flat ski, or by not being over their skis, or if they kick late, the wax is forgiving and they don't often slip. Usually, because of that extra kicker wax the skis are slower as well. But worse, many skiers begin to push backward with their skis. A tip-off is lowering the hips during the kicking motion or lack of knee compression over the lead foot. Another result is a slower tempo.

With continued skiing like this the skier gets into a vicious circle, for the best, most powerful way to get kick, or set wax, is by using a very quick downward motion to compress the leg by bending the knee slightly over the front foot. If you use your body weight to sink back and push off your ski with that big kicker on it you will never learn to use your leg properly. Next thing, you'll want to go slightly harder or faster and will look for more wax to hold you from slipping. . . .

## Double-Poling as an End in Itself

One of the most important changes that has taken place in the racing scene has been in the area of technique. The new skis and the new waxes are much faster than before, the tracks are harder and the courses are faster. These factors lead to an increased use of the double-pole and the marathon skate. You won't see the diagonal stride used much by racers cruising the flats.

Even though you will use the single stride with diagonal poling much of the time you may want to practice your double-poling or skating for certain conditions. On gradual downhill sections of terrain, or on fast snow, the double-pole and the marathon skate are fairly easy maneuvers.

You can think of the marathon skate as a special kind of double-pole. You need some momentum to begin with, then you splay one ski to the side and push or skate off it as you double-pole. It's easier to splay the ski toward the downhill side of the track, if there is one.

The success you have with double-poling and the marathon skate will depend on your balance and strength. Some strong skiers with good balance almost throw themselves out over the lead ski, whether it's for a double-pole or a skate, both arms reaching forward, and then give a tremendous thrust with the poling motion by using their arms, shoulders and body weight. Others will not have the balance to venture so far forward.

There are lots of variations of double-poling as used by individual good skiers, but it would take too much space to describe them here. Work out whichever modification suits your style and strength.

One good hint I can give, though, is that you try to get your body weight into the poling motion. This means not pushing too hard until your arms are bent—and then, when they are bent, sort of sinking down on the poles with your weight as you push.


# UPHILL SKIING

Skiing uphill under your own steam is one of the wonders of x-c. Here is a place where the many unique features of x-c combine to give you a great deal of satisfaction. The equipment is light and allows that freedom of movement which is necessary for almost all uphill skiing. The practiced x-c'er is able to exert himself and get up hills with ease. And, finally, the properly waxed skis, or the waxless skis, provide that extra in grip, or purchase, which enables you to go straight up some of the fairly steep slopes.

There are almost as many different ways to ski uphill as there are degrees of steepness. The good skier uses different techniques with varying amounts of effort, depending on the slope. I'll hit on half a dozen of the methods.

**42. and 43.** *Synchronized marathon skate step.*

**44. and 45.** *A strong marathon skate.*

## Using the Diagonal Stride

If the uphill slope is relatively flat and your skis grip well, and if there's a good track and you're feeling strong, you can glide up the hill using the plain, old, on-the-flat, diagonal technique. To get some glide going uphill takes quite a bit of strength, and sometimes it's helpful to assume a slightly crouched body position.

Be careful not to sit back in your crouch here, though: Your weight should be forward for maximum purchase. Failing to keep the body weight forward is one of the most common faults of skiers going uphill.

### BOUNDING—MORE, OR LESS

If the slope is steeper—but not so steep that you have to sidestep or herringbone—there are several techniques that may serve.

---

### THE MARATHON SKATE

The marathon skate step has made a spectacular appearance in a very short time. Some U.S. racers picked it up in Sweden in the early '80s when they were competing in a river race. (Now there's a flat course!) The local Swedes were using this hitherto unseen maneuver to dust off our skiers, who felt burdened by the one-step double-pole. Our boys brought it back to the United States and started using it frequently in 1982, including the World Championships. Some rather heated arguments on high levels followed. Officials of the FIS wanted to outlaw the skate. Some Scandinavians said that if one wanted to use the skating step he should go to the ice-skating rink, etc.

A rule was finally passed recently forbidding the step during the last 200 meters of a race. This rule was a compromise to the Scandinavians, most of whom wanted skating outlawed totally. It's ironic that a Norwegian, Ove Aunli, was disqualified in the Olympic 15 km race for skating during the last 200 meters. He might otherwise have finished fifth.

At this writing the skate is coming on stronger than ever. The Scandinavians, perhaps figuring if you can't beat 'em you'd better join 'em, are using it to great advantage and many people think that waxing of racing skis will go right out the window in the near future. Racers will develop such a strong skate that they will use only glide wax, to help make them go fast. They'll skate the uphills until they can't go any farther, then will use the herringbone. They'll skate all the flats and the tops of the uphills to gain speed.

Meanwhile, I'm still recommending that we normal folk use wax, or good waxless skis, to help us along.

The most energetic is the bounding stride used by racers when they're in a hurry. They practically leap from one ski forward onto the other. The amount of extension depends on the slope, the skier's strength and his wax; but in general he extends less than in his diagonal stride on the flat.

## THE SHUFFLE

The shuffle, long regarded by racers and coaches as used only by skiers with poor balance, is back. The reason for this is that the shuffle is one of the best ways to get up most hills. It's a rudimentary movement, perhaps one you used when you began skiing.

I can give you a few hints about this technique but you'll have to make the fine adjustments yourself after some experimenting. First, be sure the slope of the hill is not too steep and that your skis have good purchase. Then, standing fairly direct over your skis, shuffle along, trying to keep the skis in maximum contact with the snow. Concentrate on driving, or shoving, the legs ahead—one at a time, of course. Naturally, you will have to set your wax or your waxless ski bottoms with the shuffle of each forward ski, and to do this may require a slight movement, or compression of the leg, and some coordinated poling action. But the trick is to avoid as many bouncing up-and-down motions as possible. If your skis are holding well, jumping up and down on them as in ski-bounding just wastes energy.

It also helps to have fairly limber skis when doing this maneuver—another vote for those soft skis.

If you are waxing up for a long tour, a good guide to use is the shuffle. If your wax enables you to shuffle, you'll probably be O.K. for the trip.

## DOG-TROT

The third method, which I'll call the dog-trot, is good for fairly steep slopes. In this one you lean forward a bit more, assume a fairly low body position, and take rather short steps.

The key to this dog-trot is a "soft" ski out front. By that, I mean you cushion the step by bending the ankle and the knee. The knee should be right over, or even ahead of, the foot. It's as if you're sneaking up the hill, or you're trotting along on a bunch of fresh eggs, trying not to break them. It's important to keep your body weight forward. If you get back on your heels and have to rock forward onto the ball of your foot in each step, you'll soon get tired.

The poles should be used with a minimum effort. If it is necessary to pole hard with each step, or to hold yourself from slipping with each step, then (a) you should be using another technique, or (b) you need more purchase, or (c) your weight is back too far, or (d) you're not doing it right in the first place. The poles should be used almost as an afterthought.

**46–53.** *A strong stride is exhibited here on an uphill section of track.*

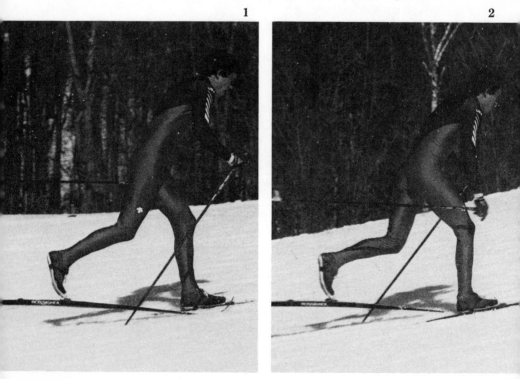

Another way of thinking about it is to imagine yourself running, or dog-trotting, up an inclined cement ramp, with sneakers on. If you wanted to jog up the ramp in the most relaxed manner, how would you do it? Chances are you'd dog-trot.

## Sidestep

The sidestep is a sure, easy way to climb. Stand with your skis across the slope, or at right angles to the fall-line. (The fall-line is the route a ball would take if it could roll freely and unimpeded down the hill, which means it's the most direct way up a slope.)

Then lift the uphill ski and move it up the hill a foot or so, digging in the uphill edge as you put it down. Now lift the other ski, place it beside the upper one—and you should be a little closer to the top of the hill. Continue.

## Traverse

The traverse is probably the tourskier's most common method of getting up hills. It is really nothing more than a diagonal, or single, stride with a bit of the sidestep effect thrown in.

Skiing up a slope with linked traverses is similar to taking a zigzag road to the top of a mountain. To start traversing, get crossways to the fall-line and, as you move your uphill ski forward in the single stride, slide it slightly up the hill; then slide the other ski alongside and ahead. Thus you proceed forward across the slope and upward at the same time. The poling motion is identical with the diagonal stride.

To change direction, link one traverse with another by getting into a herringbone position (described below) and sort of crabbing your way around. Or, you can do a kickturn. Then start upward across the slope again.

## Herringbone

The herringbone is a very quick, but tiring, method of getting up hills that are too steep for your diagonal stride.

Your legs and arms alternate, exactly as in the diagonal, but there are some important differences. First, there's no glide (unless you're a superman!); second, your skis are splayed out in a "V"—which, repeated, produces a herringbone pattern, hence the name; and third, in order to hold from slipping, you must really dig in with the inside edge of each ski.

**54.** *The herringbone.*

If you're strong and in a hurry, this is it. (It is a very important racing technique, since many of the hills on a competition course are so steep. The U.S. Team even has dry-land drills for this one.)

**AND WHEN ALL ELSE FAILS . . .**

As a last resort, you can always take off your skis and walk. Don't laugh. I've been in races when I was so tired and my wax was so bad that I know my times would have been faster if I'd taken off my skis and walked. I would have been disqualified of course, so I grunted it.

But you don't have to keep 'em on. You're out for fun, and x-c is your own thing. Right?

# DOWNHILL SKIING

As I said in Chapter One, there is a new wave of enthusiasm for cross-country downhill skiing and Telemarking. Many skiers are really into this.

Ski factories are producing new model skis that are wider than most x-c skis and have steel edges. These skis are really a cross between present day Alpine and cross-country skis. The skiers often use touring boots and three-pin bindings and sometimes refer to themselves as three-pin skiers. An added equipment feature is a heel fixture which helps lateral stability when making an Alpine turn but allows the heel to lift when making strides or Telemark turns.

Skeptics of this sport claim that these fellows are simply reinventing downhill skiing because they take lifts to mountaintops and then just ski back down.

I have had good background in Alpine skiing and always knew that in good conditions the expert skiers can make any turns on cross-country skis, even before the advent of the present specialty skis. You do everything just like you do on Alpine skis. This is not a revelation. But the cross-country downhill fans are enthused about their sport because you can also do Telemark turns, which the Alpinists can't, and you can take tours in the bargain. It's the best of both worlds, they claim.

No matter how you feel, the sport is gaining wide recognition and many contests are currently scheduled for these skiers.

I'm not going into Alpine turns, or cross-country downhill. There is plenty of material in the literature, lots of Alpine instructors and ski schools out there, and if you want to pursue this angle you can get plenty of help.

Instead, I will address the situations where you might be on a trail, with or without tracks, or on your own on the side of a mountain, and are using the more standard x-c skis. I'll cover trail skiing first.

## The Trail: Straight Down

The fastest, easiest way is straight down. Assume a relaxed, upright position, with weight evenly distributed on both skis; keep flat-footed—and go. If you want some extra speed you can crouch over and rest your forearms on the tops of your knees. This tuck cuts down wind resistance and is also restful.

Be careful of the tuck when the slope is bumpy, however, because it's a hard position to hold if you're bouncing around. On rough going, it's better to straighten up. But don't be stiff and rigid: Relax.

It's possible to go very fast on x-c skis. In races, on some steep downgrades, x-c skiers get going at least 70 kilometers per hour (about 42 mph), but

**55.** *What goes up must come down, but not necessarily in a crouch.*

you can be sure they've got their eye on a nice outrun at the bottom.
I'm not recommending such speed for you. I do say, though, that you
should always be able to see your outrun when you're going straight
down a hill—otherwise you may be headed for trouble and not know it.

Because it's no good to take a chance on bumping into something like
a tree or another skier, you'll need a few other methods of controlling
your speed and direction of travel. Like the following.

## The Trail: Step Turn

The step, or skate, turn is the most efficient method of changing direction
in any kind of skiing on any kind of skis. Just raise one ski slightly off
the snow, point it in the direction you want to go, set it down, lift the
other and bring it alongside the first.

Naturally, the faster you are going the faster you have to move those
skis. In fact, some x-c runners often practice high-speed turns by jumping
off the snow with both skis and landing with them pointed in a different
direction. This can be difficult, but it's a very neat way to change direction.

**56–59.** *Step turns can be made challenging if you try to stay with the person on the inside.*

**60.** *A snowplow, with the ski tips too far apart.*

## The Trail: Snowplow Turn

Snowplowing is possible under most conditions and it has the advantage of being more controlled than straight downhill skiing: You control not only your speed, but also your direction.

In doing the straight-down snowplow, be sure to keep the tips of your skis fairly close together while pushing your ski tails apart in order to get that edging or braking action. To turn from this position, weight or push harder on one ski, and this force will drive you around in the desired direction.

There are a couple of more informal ways to slow down which I'll cover in a minute. Meanwhile let's hit the open slopes.

## Open Slope: Traversing Down

Naturally, when you have a whole hillside to yourself you can use all the turns mentioned so far. And there's a special beauty, too. With so much more freedom of movement here, you can lay your own course between and around obstacles, and there are no compulsory corners.

Absolutely the most pleasurable way I know of for going downhill in open terrain is by using the traverse. I like to head down at an angle just steep enough to keep me going. This way, I get the maximum distance out of the slope in return for whatever climb I made up to the start of the downhill piece. I recommend it as effortless, ideal for easy step-turning, and giving you the bonus of time to enjoy the scenery as you go. And it's so quiet.

**61.** *A parallel turn in corn snow.*

## Open Slope: Telemark Turn

The Telemark turn is very graceful and most appropriate for powder skiing. It was developed long before the present-day resort slopes were packed out with such maddening efficiency. So the Telemark nearly went out of style when the Alpine boots and bindings became so restrictive as to prohibit its use (you need that heel-lifting freedom you get with x-c gear). Then, only a few x-c skiers carried on the tradition for years. But now, with many more x-c'ers skiing everywhere, including the x-c downhill crowd, I'm happy to say that this classic turn is coming back.

To do it, slide one ski ahead of the other as you go downhill. Slide it so that the binding of the forward ski is about alongside the tip of the following ski. Then stem the forward ski—to the left if it's your right ski that is ahead—weight it or edge it slightly, use your arms for balance, and you should go around. Bring your skis together to complete the turn.

One thing the Telemark has in common with other Alpine turns is controversy regarding its execution. Many skiers will insist on keeping your arms low throughout the turn while others keep them fairly high. But the beauty of the turn is in the challenge.

Don't worry if you fall. It happens all the time. But after you master this turn and can link a number of them together going down a slope, you will be something to behold.

The turn can be done at very low speeds. At higher speeds it's a bit more difficult. And, as I said, it's great for powder skiing.

## But Anything That Works Is O.K., Really

Since writing the first book I have heard of a few, but very few, broken-bone accidents in x-c skiing—one in particular being a collision between two skiers. But bone breaks are still very rare. Usually the equipment breaks before a leg gets enough stress to do so. This is a marvelous safety feature in x-c, because new equipment is a lot cheaper than doctors' fees.

Your gear will survive informal maneuvers, however, like the following. Even pride won't suffer—if you keep loose.

**62.** *A Telemark turn in powder snow.*

**63.** *Vintage shot. Old picture of U.S. Ski Team practicing synchronized double-poles.*

**64.** *And the diagonal. All together now!*

**THE BUSH-GRAB**

A friend of mine has developed a technique that's probably unique among ardent x-c'ers for negotiating some of the slopes around Vermont. He is an acrophobiac of the first order and, short of going downhill blindfolded, has perfected the bush-grab. Carefully he gauges his speed so that, when he gets near enough to the first bush on his course, he can grab it and come to a stop. He then heads off for the next bush or tree. After a trip through tree country he comes in covered with twigs and birchbark, pleased as Punch with himself and the world.

It's good to report that, as the years go by, he's cut down on the number of these braking stops.

**THE SIT-DOWN**

If you get in trouble downhill, don't be too proud to sit down and scoot on your fanny to a stop. Start by easing your weight down so you can drag your hands in the snow on each side—like twin stabilizers—to keep from tipping over sideways. Then gradually let your body sink into the snow, slightly back and to one side or the other. Once I hit the snow I imagine I'm sliding into home.

Safe!

---

### GETTING UP FROM A FALL

Some people have difficulty getting up from a fall or are afraid to fall. In either case, skiing is made less enjoyable—which is too bad. Because almost all falls in x-c are O.K. They don't hurt. In fact, you can gain a certain confidence in falling without fear if you do fall occasionally. I'm not telling you to rush out and take a winder; but if you are a worrier, try to change your attitude. When you do fall remind yourself that it wasn't too bad after all.

Getting up from a fall is easy. First, if necessary, you should untwist yourself, then get your skis together and pointed in the same direction. To do this you may have to lie on your back and swing your skis over you up in the air, keeping them parallel. If you're on a slope be sure your skis end up below you and across the hill.

Next, hunch up a bit, or assume a fetal position, then get on your knees and push yourself up with your hands, which are braced against the snow or against your skis.

It is often a mistake to try to hoist yourself using your poles. This becomes too much like a difficult pull-up, or the poles sink and you slither back down onto the snow. You might even want to take off your poles before you get up.

# 5

# X-C for the Handicapped

AS CROSS-COUNTRY SKIING GROWS, you can expect to hear more and more about skiing for the handicapped. My first contact with their participation in snow sports was watching amputees zooming down some Alpine slopes with their outriggers: you may have seen some of them, too, at least on TV. I'll confess I didn't think much about how the handicapped could ski x-c until I came up with some very minor injuries and was faced with the prospect of not being able to ski for a while myself. Then I was pleasantly surprised to find what I could do with my leg in a cast.

Since then I have run into more and more handicapped skiers and am happy to report that x-c is well suited for them. In fact, the handicapped often develop so strong a desire to ski and exercise that their attitude could be the envy of many racers in training.

I hope my observations and the information I include here will provide just another spur in the development of skiing, x-c especially, for the handicapped.

## Amputees

Most people agree that below-the-knee amputees can perform quite well on x-c skis. There is little question that Alpine skiing with outriggers on each arm—ski poles with very short skis on the bottoms instead of baskets and points—plus the aid of gravity, make this an easier sport than x-c, but if you're an amputee and want to do x-c, you'll be able to.

Above-the-knee amputees unquestionably will have more difficulties, and should start out on very easy terrain. After that, several factors will enter into determining what can be accomplished—the natural ability and strength of the skier, snow conditions, the track itself, the terrain, and so on.

Again, in general, Alpine skiing will be easier for most amputees since the overall level of conditioning is not so high as that required for x-c. Some amputee Alpinists consider themselves as skiing better than 70 percent of the physically normal skiing population—and with good reason.

## The Blind

There are some good programs for the blind, a few of which I will describe below. Suffice it to say that almost all blind people need a guide to accompany them: It's a one-on-one situation. I say "almost all blind people" because there are some skiers who know certain courses well enough to be able to tour 10–15 kilometers on their own. And you may have already guessed another vital need for blind skiers: good, deep tracks which serve to guide the skis.

It's pretty hard to imagine yourself in the position of a handicapped person unless you are one. But here is a situation you can simulate, slightly. Just put on a blindfold next time you're out and see what it's like to ski this way. If you do this and think it's difficult, then try to imagine how it would be if you had balance problems in addition, as many blind people do.

Guides or instructors for the blind are often blindfolded as part of their training. In this way they can understand the problems better, and thus can communicate better with their students.

### THE PARTIALLY-SIGHTED

The partially-sighted have approximately the same needs as the blind in order to ski x-c. However, they are judged to have some advantages over the blind and, in most of the races they run in, they are put in a separate division.

It's generally agreed that skiing x-c is easier for the blind or partially-sighted than skiing Alpine.

## Paraplegics

The Boston Marathon has featured a special Wheelchair Division in this, the most famous marathon run in the United States. In 1977 the wheelchair entries started 15 minutes ahead of the field and the winner arrived at the finish having been passed by *only 30* runners.

I never imagined that paraplegics could do anything comparable on x-c skis but there are specially made fiberglass sleds which serve the same purpose as a wheelchair. The skiers use shortened poles and propel themselves around with tremendous double-poling. In some competitions

**65. and 66.** *The Ski for Light program. Blind skiers with their guides.*

**67.** *Pulk skier Richard Brunvand, a paraplegic from Ann Arbor, Michigan, competing in the 1979 Ski for Light program in Squaw Valley, California.*

the paraplegics have more than held their own against racers with other handicaps, such as blindness.

PARAPARETICS

There is not much information or experience I can report about paraparetics—people who have partial paralysis of the legs—but in talking with some who ski Alpine, they sound confident about wanting to do x-c.

In the meantime, I would appreciate any information you can send me.

## The Deaf

Skiing x-c may seem like a straightforward situation if you're deaf, but it's not all clear sailing. The way one paraparetic explained it to me exemplifies the fine attitude displayed by so many of the handicapped: "Boy, am I glad I'm not deaf, because so many of those people have equilibrium problems!"

There are many x-c races scheduled for the deaf; in fact, many deaf skiers enter regularly sanctioned races in the United States. The distinguishing mark of a deaf skier is a special armband, and the signal for passing—if you happen to be fast enough—is tapping his ski pole with yours instead of shouting *"Track!"*

## Ready to Help

Most handicapped people snort at anyone who even begins to feel sorry for them; this is especially true of those who get deeply involved in sports and recreation. Some studies show that involvement in these areas helps to produce a very high level of success in professional occupations like medicine, law, etc.

But then there are the handicapped who either do not know of the possibilities open to them, or who are reluctant to try something in sports, for instance. These are the people who need encouragement and this is one reason I give a list of organizations to contact right here.

*Note:* To date there are not many full-fledged programs for instructing handicapped in x-c. Many experts feel that the handicapped themselves will eventually become the best teachers, but there have not been good training programs for them. In the meantime there is a need for instruction and if you are interested you should get in touch with one of the organizations listed below and offer your services.

*National Handicapped Sports and Recreation Association,* 10085 West 18th Ave., Lakewood, Colorado 80215.

Among other things, this organization sponsors the National Handicapped Skiers Championships. The first x-c race in this yearly series was held in 1978 at Winter Park, Colorado.

*Blind Organization for Leisure Development* (BOLD), 533 East Main Street, Aspen, Colorado 81611.

BOLD was founded by Jean Eymere, a former member of the French Olympic Alpine Team. Jean is a diabetic who lost his sight and then decided to promote Alpine skiing for the blind.

*Ski for Light,* 1455 West Lake Street, Minneapolis, Minnesota 55408.

Ski for Light is an outreach organization of the Sons of Norway. The Sons of Norway now has 105,000 members and 340 lodges in North America and are well known for their Ski for Light programs, both regional and international.

In the x-c races they organize for the blind, each blind skier has a guide or instructor who works with him in preparation for the race. They practice on the course—which has two parallel tracks so they can ski side by side—and work out audible signals for the race.

One official of Ski for Light commented that the most significant aspect of Ski for Light is that the guides and organizers are working with handicapped people, not for them. The sighted guides benefit as much or more than the disabled people they are working with.

Mike Gallagher, present coach of the U.S. Ski Team, was race chief for the 1977 running, held at Woodstock, Vermont. In commenting on the race Mike said he was amazed at the speeds attained by the blind

**68. and 69.** *If you have skied much downhill in deep, icy tracks, you know that it's possible to attain very high speeds and have difficulty even getting out of the tracks to snowplow. You usually end up hanging on for your life—or bailing out of the tracks and taking your chances in the crust at the side. The first time I saw the drags pictured here was on a trip to Germany in 1977 (where these photos were taken) and I must admit there were some times when I wished I had them. The ski instructor put these rigs on his skis (68, above) at binding level. There is a spring-loaded hinge which keeps the claws, or drags, in place during normal skiing. But when he wants to slow up—as on a fast downhill—he simply pulls the cords (69, below), which are attached to the claws. The harder he pulls, the more drag he gets and the slower he goes. I don't think many racer types will take to these, but then there are always the rest of us. These contraptions could be used to fine advantage by anyone with a lower-body handicap, or by everybody who's leery of fast downhill stretches.*

70. *Canadian Association for Disabled skiing event.*

skiers. He cited one or two cases where the guides got in over their heads and couldn't keep up with the handicapped racers.

At this race there were 91 entries, divided into three classes: blind, partially-sighted, and physically (motor) handicapped. There were only two in the physically handicapped class but one was a paraplegic who won his division handily and defeated over half the field as well. His equipment was a fiberglass sled, shortened poles—and a pair of superstrong arms.

The interest in this whole program has grown, with 25 Ski for Light programs being held annually in the United States and Canada. You can get more information from the address above. In Canada, contact the *Canadian Association of Disabled Skiing,* Box 307, Kimberley, B.C. V1A 2Y9, Canada.

Finally there is the *U.S. Deaf Skiers Association.* For information write Donald Fields, President, 159 Davis Avenue, Hackensack, New Jersey 07601; or Ellen Roth, 56 W. 84th Street, New York, New York 10024.

For leads to counterparts of these groups in the Dominion, write to *Cross-Country Canada,* 333 River Road, Ottawa, Ontario K1L 8H9, Canada.

# 6

# Kid Stuff

LOTS OF QUERIES COME TO ME from parents who want to know how to get their kids into x-c skiing. No two family situations are exactly alike, of course, so it's hard to prescribe any standard approach, but I'll summarize some of my observations and experiences. For a more detailed or specialized approach, I refer you to some of the books listed in the References.

## Advantages

The advantages of getting kids into x-c should be pretty obvious:

1. *X-C skiing is a natural activity for children.* It's the next thing to walking, and chances are that kids don't have hang-ups about balance, or fear of falling, etc.
2. *X-C is very learnable compared to Alpine skiing.* After a few minutes, or a few times out, most kids will be on their way to a workable competence.
3. *X-C can be immediate.* If you live near snow you can go out with practically no fuss and bother—which means that kids often get a chance to capitalize on their current whims or desires.
4. *X-C is more available than Alpine skiing.* If you can find some snow almost anywhere, x-c is go. No lift tickets to buy; no wait at lift-lines.
5. *X-C equipment, being more flexible and comfortable than Alpine gear, makes x-c more attractive to kids.* And a x-c outfit is much less expensive.

## Philosophy and Guidelines

The basic approach should be to make it fun for kids. Every time you plan something for a youngster, or a group of youngsters, ask yourself how you can make it fun. If your primary concern is getting kids out of the house for a while, or if x-c for them is some part of a baby-sitting arrangement, you probably are on the wrong track.

My mother-in-law once asked me when I thought kids ought to start skiing and I told her, "Just before they learn to walk; that way they won't develop any bad habits in form."

Well, I was putting her on a little. But we did get our children going as soon as we could, and in all cases they were clomping on skis around the living room floor well before age two.

You might not be in the right circumstances to do anything like this so I'll suggest that you start your kids on x-c skiing as soon as you can find equipment for them.

### FOR LITTLE ONES

With very young kids—from age two up to eight or ten—it's important to make x-c skiing a family thing. You know how kids are, often in need of a parent or an older brother or sister to help them out. Most of them are accustomed to having some family member around at all times and it's only natural to have it that way when they ski.

Make x-c skiing an adventure for kids. There are all sorts of games you can play, depending on their age. Hide-and-seek may sound a bit corny to an adult since it's pretty clear that anyone can follow ski tracks and find someone who is hiding. But that's just the point. The little kids really love something like this—for many it's a discovery, and they learn in the process.

So almost any game you play on foot will adapt itself to x-c. Just go slowly with it, assuring some degree of success for the kids who are playing the game, and chances are they'll enjoy it.

### FOR SCHOOL AGE

As kids get older you can take them on short jaunts. Anytime you can inject a practical element or a goal into a situation, you have a good thing. We used to ski over to visit a neighbor who had invited us for a little party. And our kids actually skied to school—I know this is one of those things you read about and never quite believe, but it was a case of their skiing or our having to drive them. They liked school, so you can imagine I tried to make sure their skis were well waxed every day for the trip.

This introduces a couple of other concepts. In skiing to school our kids acquired a certain degree of independence, they overcame the vagaries

**71.** *Parental involvement: go along, encourage, and keep a light touch.*

of all sorts of weather, and they gained confidence in plain x-c skiing and in their ability to master physical activities. They also learned that x-c skiing is practical.

In setting up x-c skiing for kids you will discover increasing opportunities to pose a challenge for them that they will delight in meeting. It can take the form of skiing to school, going on a tour through hitherto unknown terrain to a friend's house, an inn, another ski area, a lean-to, a picnic site, a good view, a cabin, and so on.

Through it all, keep this x-c thing low-key. So the kids didn't want to ski to school one day? No big deal—pack 'em in the car and drive them.

Or they didn't want to go touring. That's O.K., too. Next time just try to make their x-c experience something they will enjoy more and will want to do again. You know how kids are: If something is fun, they'll do it.

## How to Begin

Kids will need a lot of attention getting started in x-c. However, it's not necessarily instruction they'll need. In fact, I've advised a lot of parents not to try and teach their kids, or not to let their kids see them ski too much for fear the kids might pick up bad habits. Give the kids assurance; watch them, encourage them, cheer them on. This will do more than anything else in the beginning.

But above all, don't *hover*. Don't give them the idea you're riding herd on them—or that they've got to please you, for heaven's sake! Heavy-handed parental gung-ho can ruin any sport for a kid. So when I say "watch them," I mean to be always available to encourage the child who wants you to.

Start on the flats and gradual downhills. Walk along with them, prop them up, or straddle them with your legs and guide them. Uphills will be a problem, but if you are patient with them on the flats and downs for a while, even pulling them back up the hills, soon you will be rewarded and they will do the uphills by themselves. Next thing you know they will be skiing away from you and asking why you are so slow. Naturally, having waxless skis—or waxed skis that work—is important for the uphills.

Probably the best single piece of instruction you *can* give them is how to get up from a fall. As soon as kids are confident that they can get up themselves they'll be a long way toward skiing on their own. But until then they will get stuck in all sorts of awkward situations and will need help. One year one of our kids had boots that were too big and every time she fell down she came right out of them (the ultimate in safety features!). Since she didn't yet know how to put on her own boots this did cause a problem. You see, we did start them young.

If the skis are short, as I advised, kids will be able to roll right over on their backs, flipping their skis overhead and bringing them together. If they flop the skis downhill, or below them, and then get on to their knees, they will be able to push themselves back into a standing position. If they want to use their poles to hoist themselves up, that's fine, but it's not necessary. It may be easier without poles.

If kids have a chance to observe good skiers, just to see how it's done, they'll catch on. They are marvelous mimics. So I wouldn't advise any formal class instruction for them until they are fairly well advanced in technique, or just yearning for instruction. The best thing they can do is play games, take small trips, have fun fooling around and playing follow-the-leader, and being in an unstructured situation.

There is an increasing number of good x-c films out now and showing these to kids is another way to improve their skill and enjoyment of the sport.

## The Bill Koch League

For several years the Eastern Ski Division of the U.S. Ski Association has sponsored a league for kids' Nordic skiing—that is, in jumping and x-c. The original league was named after Torger Tokle, a famous ski-jumper who was killed during the Second World War serving in the U.S. 10th Mountain Division in Italy. After Bill Koch's Olympic silver medal in 1976 the name of the league was changed to recognize his feat.

Many teams in the league are well organized and coached. They begin training during the fall, have fund-raising drives to buy equipment, and in general go the club route.

Parental involvement can be very constructive here. After all, someone has to help drive the kids to meets, pick up their bibs, wax the skis, get the kids organized, and so on. In fact, even during some of the training sessions we find parents right up there in the workouts, learning such things as hill-bounding, roller-skiing, and specificity exercises. During the summers some parents lead trips in the mountains. All this is good.

I hope the league stays this way and that it remains low-key and that the race schedules don't get too imposing. I worry about the "Little League Baseball syndrome"—parents screaming at their kids, at the umps, at the coaches, and all that. The minute ski parents get competitive, or worry too much about their kids' times, or insist on certain training sessions, or get upset about missing the wax, there's going to be a bummer.

## Technique Competitions

In our area we have had good success with technique competitions for the younger age groups. No times are necessary. We assign numbers to

**72.** *National Team members often coach at junior camps . . . like this one in Putney, Vermont.*

the competitors and this immediately gives them a sense that something special is going on. Then we ask each competitor to report to each of several stations for some brief instruction or explanation about a certain skiing maneuver, i.e., diagonal technique, one-step double-poling, skating, etc. When the competitor feels comfortable enough to perform he is judged and assigned style points from 1 to 5, or 1 to 10, and then moves off to the next station. And so on.

**73.** *Youngsters registering at a station for instruction and technique competition.*

There are several winners in this situation. The kids learn something about technique and their scores may entice them to practice certain maneuvers more, after the event. In addition, the instructors—teen-agers are the best ones to use—gain a lot from this experience of coaching and judging. If you ever want to learn something just put yourself in a situation where you have to teach it. Amazing what that will do to get you pumped up.

The most important thing to remember is that x-c is a marvelous lifetime sport. Let's not do anything to discourage anyone from enjoying it as a recreation.

# 7

# Waxing

THE WAXING OF X-C skis used to be one of the great mysteries of skiing. Few newcomers to the sport could understand how any substance applied to a ski bottom would enable one to go *up* a hill. And of the people who did accept this notion, few knew what waxes to use or how to apply them. It was no wonder that many skiers were turned away from cross-country skiing.

Many of the competitive groups did little to help the situation either, keeping secret, with a skill to be envied by the CIA, their special wax combinations used for races. Some teams hired wax experts for the bigger, more important races, virtually locking these wizards away in isolation for many hours before the meet. No movie-going or bar-hopping the night before, not by a long shot.

This whole situation changed very gradually, and a few years ago, just before the advent of fiberglass and waxless skis, things seemed to have leveled off. Most x-c'ers were taking to waxing and doing a reasonably good job. There were lots of treatises on the subject and even more waxes available. Waxing had almost become an accepted part of the sport.

But now we're off and flying again—in many different directions. There are large numbers of waxless skis, manufactured and homemade, some of which you can wax; there are wooden skis with wood bottoms or plastic bottoms; and finally, there are plastic skis with different bottoms.

The total amount of knowledge necessary to be able to wax every type of x-c ski in any condition has increased several times in just a few years. Fortunately, however, the physical process of applying wax is getting easier and easier. So if you are content with taking the simplest approach to waxing and if you stick with just one kind of ski, then it becomes easier than ever before. On the other hand, if you are waxing for a competitive event you'll virtually need a computer to handle all the different possibilities.

I'll hit the basics for you and then will mention some of the refinements used by top competitive skiers.

**Waxing Waxless, Too?**

In earlier editions I separated the waxing of waxless skis from the waxing of waxable skis. Now, in a sense, it's become simplified. You wax all skis using the same methods.

What's happened? You thought you didn't have to wax waxless skis. The term, waxless ski, is getting more and more misleading. All the experts I talk with, including many waxless ski company officials, say it's a good idea to wax waxless skis with speed wax on the tips and tails. In fact, some waxless skis are designed for waxing even under the foot, just like waxable skis.

Waxless skis are getting better and better all the time. Some manufacturers of waxless skis, in looking for the best performance possible, have designed their skis for waxing in certain conditions. No waxless ski I have used is well-suited for all conditions and the companies who suggest waxing are simply admitting this and trying to help you with your skiing.

So before you buy a waxless ski, be sure you are thoroughly familiar with the base and its characteristics. Some waxless skis, particularly those with machined designs in the bottoms, are not suited for kicker, or grip, waxing. Others are designed for waxing.

Still, you should use speed wax regularly on tip and tail sections that do not contain a machined design. Speed wax will make the skis slide forward easier and it will also help to protect the bottom surface from wear and oxidation.

In this chapter I'll talk about the main factors in any waxing situation: those are the method of application, the choice of wax, and the variables.


# APPLYING SPEED WAX

Before you start any waxing, be sure your skis are clean and dry. No wax will work well if it is put on over little flecks of dirt and water. In fact, most waxes won't even stick to a wet surface.

The method most often used for applying speed wax in cake form is to rub it on. Corking the wax to smooth it is O.K., but again, don't speed wax the area under the foot where you plan to use kicker wax in the case of waxable skis, or the section of your waxless ski under the foot if waxing there will interfere with the purchase ability of the ski.

If you have an iron handy and want to drip the cake wax on, then iron and scrape (as described in Chapter 2). This is fine. You'll be best off doing this in a warm room.

You can use spray waxes almost anywhere. They are the easiest to apply. They are also the most expensive. And you had better not let many of the ozone group see you discharging that stuff into the atmosphere.

## IRONING IN WAX FOR SPEED

I was skiing competitively at Dartmouth College when the Olympic Alpine team returned in 1948 with a new method of waxing their skis. It was called ironing! We rubbed stuff like Sohm's Red Wax on our downhill skis and then ironed it smooth for speed. It was a major advance.

Very soon after that, perhaps during the same season, we began to wax differently for slalom than for downhill. For the lowspeed events like slalom where acceleration was important, we ironed the wax. For the faster events like downhill we painted wax on in overlapping steps, beginning at the tail of the ski. These steps were designed to break the suction between the snow and the skis and many was the time when we could feel that release at certain speeds. It was almost the same feeling you get when a car shifts into overdrive.

Many of the theories that pertain today were in use back then. We used longer, thinner steps for cold, powdery snow, and thicker, shorter steps to break the suction on wet snow.

In the mid-fifties, when I was coaching four events, I used paint jobs on the tips and tails of our x-c skis and it worked wonderfully well. In one race, our team's skis were so fast that all the racers fell down at the bottom of one hill because they weren't used to the speed. I don't know if we gained any time overall.

All this happened with wood skis. The shift to fiberglass skis most of you know about. Painting wax on skis was discontinued after a while because it was found that ironing and scraping was easier and faster. And so we come to the present period, but it's not over by any means.

The latest trick in the big leagues is to treat your ski bottom using many of the principles that have always guided us. For instance, if you want a fast base for very cold snow you sand the bottom with very fine sandpaper, sometimes 320 or 420 grit. And if you want a fast base for very wet snow, where you might encounter water in the tracks, you gouge out the bottom with a file or some other tool, putting longitudinal furrows—to be sure, they are very small furrows—there so the water will have someplace to flow without causing so much suction between the snow and the ski. Some companies prepare the bottoms on klister skis for you. It's the same idea you see advertised for tires which supposedly operate effectively on wet highways.

What's next? It's probably time to recycle a few of these ideas but we'll have to wait and see what happens.

## Two Exceptions

Waxless skis sometimes ice up in variable conditions, especially when there is water in the track. To help prevent this it is a good idea to spray the kicker section with WD-40, or some silicone compound. This will not interfere significantly with your purchase and it will diminish the icing problem.

In very cold conditions with waxable skis most knowledgeable waxers cover tips and tails with a hard wax designed for cold weather rather than using speed wax. These x-c purchase waxes are plenty fast enough, sometimes faster than any speed wax the average racing coach can concoct, and these waxes have the added advantage of providing you with more purchase.

### HOW OFTEN

Here are the ways you can tell when your skis need more speed wax:

1. Those whitish spots or streaks begin to appear on the ski bottoms, or the whole bottom takes on a paler hue.
2. You have cold-snow wax on and the weather turns warm, etc.
3. You are using the same model as someone else and your skis are a lot slower.

## Choosing Speed Wax

If you want to keep it simple, get hold of a cake of wax for cold snow and one for wet snow. If the cakes are too big to carry in your pocket while skiing, break them into smaller pieces. It doesn't take much to wax a pair of skis.

Back in my early jumping days we always used paraffin for speed. The market wasn't flooded with all the present-day varieties of Alpine waxes and spray waxes, so most of us used Lebanon White for every snow condition. When it was warm we put on a rough coat of White; when it was cold, a thin, smooth coat. Lebanon White was readily available: you see, it's nothing more than the paraffin used on preserves.

Don't laugh. I try to get my skiers to have wax boxes on their own and in a fit of generosity I often help to get their collection started by donating some Lebanon White. I still use it, just the way I did in the '40s.

You can use it, too. It's cheaper than anything on the market.

If you have a good background in Alpine waxing then you might want to get hold of several brands of speed wax and proceed from there. I don't recommend this for the average tourskier, though. The difference between a universal cold-snow wax and one more specialized according to a narrower temperature range is not that significant for touring. Keep it simple. Furthermore, waxless skis are generally slower than waxable ones, so if you want to be that much faster you should consider switching skis.

## SOME VARIABLES IN PURCHASE WAX PERFORMANCE

Before I get into this section it's a good time to address the owners of waxless skis. You may never choose to use purchase wax, no matter what model waxless ski you have. Or you may have waxless skis that are not designed for kicker wax. In either event, you can skip this whole section on purchase waxing.

If your waxless skis are designed for waxing under the foot, then you should learn from experience, or by talking with someone in the know, under what conditions you will need kicker wax.

Several years ago when x-c was new to so many people, the main consideration was getting some climb, or purchase, and it was assumed that any wax you selected would be applied to the whole ski. Today, however, waxing for purchase, kick, climb, or whatever you want to call it, is not just putting something on the ski bottoms and going out. There are several variables, and an understanding of these will help make you a better waxer.

Generally, *the thicker you apply the wax the more climb you'll get.*

### Length of Kicker Zone

The longer your kicker strip is, the more purchase you will have. The extreme is to wax the whole ski with a purchase wax, and, so long as the wax is not slow, this is fine. Lots of skiers still do this, and it offers the utmost simplicity in wax selection.

The other extreme comes from some racers who try to use as short a kicker as possible, sometimes on the order of 20 centimeters (8 inches). This way they can use speed wax on the rest of the ski and be faster on the downhills.

The use of purchase wax, or fast x-c wax, on the whole ski *vs* hot-waxing the tips and tails with Alpine wax, is one of the debates going on now in the racing world. In general, not much, if anything, is gained by using Alpine wax on tips and tails in very cold, powder conditions. Many racers dispense with the Alpine wax and use some brand of very hard cold weather x-c wax. One claim for using this x-c wax is that it makes the skis more stable in the track.

**Ski Flex**

Some skis are stiffer than others and this flex plays a vital part in the performance of any wax job. Just imagine a ski so stiff that when you press down on the mid-section, where you have waxed for purchase, it does not come in contact with the snow! You won't get much climb with *this* ski.

It follows that your ski should be the right flex for you (see how to test for flexibility in Chapter 1). If it is too stiff, you will need a longer kicker strip and a thicker coat. If it is too limber, you will not need so much wax—but it will wear off more easily. If you are not a serious racer it's much better to have a ski that is too limber rather than one too stiff.

It's easy to be influenced by racers' skis, which are usually a fair amount stiffer than those used by recreational skiers of the same size. Racers are stronger and can more easily use a stiff ski. Their klister skis, for example, are so stiff that most tourskiers couldn't possibly use the kicker wax under the foot because they couldn't flatten the ski against the snow. But the racers can, when they need to. And then when they want to ride their skis, as on a downhill section, they will be using primarily the speed wax they have put on tips and tails and will be much faster than a person with limber skis whose kicker wax would provide some drag.

Leave the stiff skis to the racers.

**Skiing Technique**

Some skiers kick down very hard, while others have what I describe as a more gentle, long-drawn-out kick. The stronger skier with the harder kick generally can get away with less-thick purchase wax and a shorter strip of it. The gentler type of skier may need a longer strip of wax, but might be able to use something a bit harder or faster—assuming both skiers weigh the same and have identical skis, etc.

**Wax and Snow Conditions**

It goes without saying that your choice of purchase wax and the existing snow conditions have a lot to do with your skis' performance. Nuf sed.

## METHODS FOR APPLYING PURCHASE WAX

There are several different ways to put purchase wax on your skis. The most important consideration is getting a smooth, finished coat on a clean, dry surface. You'll soon develop a favorite method of application and should stick with it as long as it continues to work for you.

## Use of Heat with Purchase Waxes

Using heat to melt the wax, or soften it to make smoothing easier, was considered bad form by some purists several years ago. I always went ahead with heat anyway because it was a lot easier. And I never had any trouble with the wax's performance.

Now the use of heat is almost universally accepted. This doesn't mean you must use heat to wax, or that you can use it without certain precautions. If you use an iron for hard wax be sure it is just hot enough, and no more, to do the job, which is to smooth the wax out. A rough guide is to not let the wax smoke from the heat. A temperature of about 140° F/60° C—right around the *Wool* setting—is usually recommended. A too-hot iron will cause extreme melting: The wax may run into the groove (thereby causing your ski to "swim" as it fails to track straight, or causing a build-up of ice in the groove), or the wax may run over onto the edges of the ski. Also, a hot iron can damage the ski bottom. These same cautions hold true for torching any wax.

With klisters it has always been a favorite trick of mine to melt them in a pot over moderate heat and paint them on (see page 91). This is O.K., but take care that the klisters don't begin to smoke. Occasionally I've left the mixture on the stove too long and it has caught fire. Not good.

## APPLYING HARD WAX

I'll list some methods for applying hard wax and give brief descriptions of each.

*Rub and cork.* This is the standard method. Rub the wax on your kicking area, or longer if you want, and smooth it out with a cork. If you do this in a warm room you will usually have good luck in smoothing the wax. The smoother the wax the better it will perform for you, uphill and downhill.

*Rub and iron.* Rub the wax on and smooth it with an ordinary flatiron, as above, being careful not to force wax into the groove or onto the edges of the skis.

*Rub and rag.* Rub on the wax as before, then heat it with a torch and, using a rag scrunched up into a little ball, smooth the wax on one side of the ski groove, then the other. The size of the rag ball might be no bigger than is necessary to cover a dime or quarter. If it's small, it will soak up some wax, you'll have better control of it, and smoothing will be easier.

If you rub too hard you will force the wax into the groove or over onto the edge. It takes a delicate touch and most skiers enjoy this kind of art work.

*Melt and cork.* You can "melt" hard wax onto the ski bottom and then

**74. and 75.** *Ironing hard wax and what it looks like close up (75).*

cork it. Melting can take two forms: either you hold the wax against a hot iron and drip it on, or you warm the wax by holding it against an iron or near a torch, and actually rub it on. If you drip it on, it will take longer to cork in.

*Melt and rag.* As above. The most common method is to heat the wax and rub it on, then rag it in, using heat from a torch.

Some skiers use various combinations of these methods. You could rub wax on, iron it, then rag. And so on.


## APPLYING KLISTER

Klisters are the most maligned waxes in x-c. So many skiers have had problems applying klister that they have gotten discouraged and, in turn, have discouraged others about waxing in general. Poor misunderstood klisters!

With decent waxing facilities and a little practice you will be amazed both at how easy it is to apply klisters and how well they work. Klisters, by comparision, almost always climb better than hard waxes. Rarely do you slip if you have the proper klister for a given condition, whereas with the proper hard wax for a given situation, you are always bound to slip now and then, or on a steep uphill.

Here are the standard methods for applying klisters. As always, you should wax in a warm room with a warm wax, and your skis should be dry.

*Apply with heat and paint.* One neat method is to put the klister on your ski, drawing two beads for the length of your kicker strip. Then heat it gently with a torch and paint it smooth. Care must be exercised anytime you apply pressure—as with a brush—to soft wax in order to keep it from running into the groove or over the edges. Some people use a cork for smoothing.

*Apply and rub.* Apply the klister as above and then, using the meaty part of your palm right below the thumb, smooth it out. If you wax in a warm room with warm wax, no other heat should be necessary. You can probably get the best control over wax thickness, etc., using this procedure. But many people don't like to get their hands sticky and therefore shun this method. If you are one of these you can use an iron on low heat.

*Apply and smooth with a scraper.* Apply the klister as above and then use a scraper to smooth it. Some companies provide an excellent plastic scraper with every box of klister, but you can also use a metal scraper. You'll have the best luck if you work on one side of the groove, then the other. Don't pull the scraper with too much pressure or you'll spill the wax off the running surface.

*Cookpot method.* Punch a few holes in your klister tubes and throw

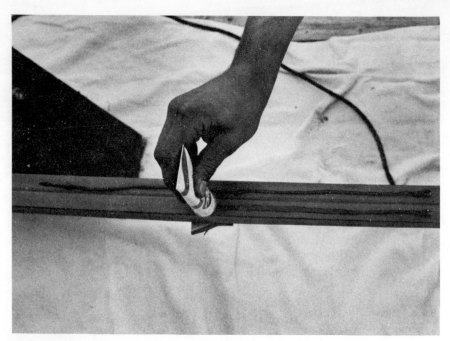

**76. and 77.** *Drawing a bead of klister on the kicker zone, then (77, below) smoothing it on with a plastic scraper.*

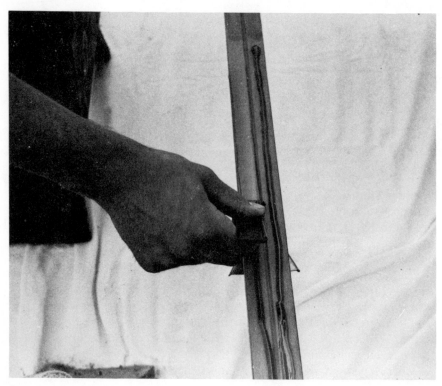

them in a pot to heat and the klister will ooze out. Grab a paintbrush and apply the wax.

The cookpot method is marvelous for applying mixes. If you want a 3-to-1 mixture of Red and Silver simply put it into the pot. This method is about the only way to klister large numbers of skis efficiently. As I advised above, heat the klister not quite to a smoking point, then take it off the heat and paint it on the ski.

## How Long and How Thick

After you have selected a kicker wax—i.e., purchase wax for the kicker zone—the main question that remains is: How long and how thick should it be?

I can give you an estimate, but you should work final details out for yourself by experimenting. Keeping a little waxing diary, or some such, will prove invaluable. Most tourskiers apply kicker wax from a point behind the heel, and going forward, up the ski toward the tip, for about 60–80 cm.

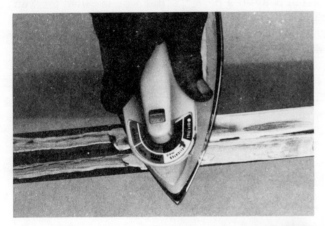

**78.** *Ironing klister.*

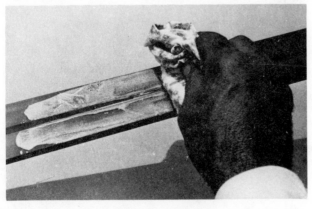

**79.** *Wiping off klister after it has been heated.*

You should experiment with kicker strips by shortening them, moving them forward or back with respect to the center of the ski, etc.

For comparison, racers these days begin waxing at the heel, or even slightly forward of that point, and use short strips, averaging from 30 to 50 cm.

There really is no firm rule for determining the thickness of a wax coat, but I always begin with an "average" coat of hard wax, which is one I can easily see after it is smoothed yet not so thick that I can scoop it off in gobs with a fingernail. Then, if I need more climb I can add more wax, making a thicker coat.

I put klister on so it's a little thicker than a good coat of paint. Usually it's better to have it thinner than thicker (see below).

## How Often

Hard waxes will last for long distances in the right conditions. I've skied over 100 km on some wax jobs.

The rule with hard waxes is easy: If the wax still works, leave it on. If it's worn off a bit, patch it up. If a newer, softer wax is called for, you can apply it directly over the old wax. If a newer, harder wax is called for, you should clean your skis and rewax.

Klisters are a bit different. They pick up dirt, bits of hemlock cones, pine needles, leaves, etc., quite easily and after most one-day trips you will have to clean them off and rewax. However, if the klister looks relatively clean and it still works, use it.

## Mixing Klisters

You can mix klisters in the pot or on the ski. I've already explained the pot method; it's amazing what you can get away with. I've seldom made

---

### HAIRIES AND WAXING

As you might have guessed already, much of the theory behind waxing applies to your Hairies. You can vary the length of the kicker zone, you can make it rough or smooth, you can use stiff skis or more limber skis, you can even scrape across the ski instead of from tip to tail, and you can use tools with different grits. Above all, you will have to experiment for yourself.

The U.S. Team is still experimenting. After their success at Falun they have had other successes, but there have been a few goof-ups, too. In some races they used the Hairies when conventional wax was the order of the day. So now they are backing off a bit, trying to find a middle ground.

**80.** *Bill Koch testing "Hairies" just before the start of the Swedish Ski Games in 1982. Dan Simoneau looks on as coach Ruff Patterson explains what's "on" each ski.*

a serious error when brewing klisters, and my success may be due to the wide range of temperature conditions that most klisters work in.

If you don't want to mix up a batch of klister in a pot, or if you like certain kinds of art work, don't hesitate to mix the wax right on your ski. Putting on a few strips of Yellow, Red, and Silver and then scraping them in together leaves a lovely colored design on your skis. That's worth something right there! (This particular combination might work well for variable, wet granular conditions, by the way.)

I've mixed about one part Purple to three or four Blue for conditions that looked straight Blue; this is a favorite.

Silver is a good toughener and I've mixed this successfully with all the other klisters. It makes the mixture last long and often will provide extra speed.

Silver is the most magical wax I know. I've even used it alone, thin, for old, cold, hard-packed powder snow. Explain that one by reading the labels!

### Two New Klister Techniques

One problem we often encounter with the softer klisters like Red and Yellow is the spreading effect. The klister, during use, oozes or rolls onto the sidewalls and occasionally causes your skis to grab when you edge them, as in doing a skate turn, or a step turn. To keep the klister from rolling over the edges it helps to first put on a very thin coat of a Blue klister. Then cover it with Red or Yellow.

Another method to help prevent this spreading is one I came up with a little while back and enjoy doing. I put a bead of Silver klister, preferably one of the harder Silvers like Rex or Rode, along each edge and smooth it to a width of about ½ cm. Then I put the day's soft klister on the rest of the ski bottom and smooth as usual. The Silver acts a bit like a dam and holds the softer klister away from the edge. Since Silver klisters are very versatile, and work in the same conditions as the Red and Yellow klisters, they never have an adverse effect on my wax job. In fact, my skis are usually a bit faster than they would be with straight Red or Yellow klister.

### Hard Wax Over Klister

This is technically one of the toughest wax jobs to put on your skis. But it's theoretically one of the easiest mixtures to understand. One set of conditions which lends itself to this combination is a hard granular track with some newer powder snow blowing in and around it. If you were to wax for the granular snow alone (with klister) it would be slow as death in the powder; if you waxed for the powder alone (with hard wax) it would soon wear off in the granular. So you compromise, and use both

klister and hard wax. If it were fairly cold you could put on some Blue
Klister in the usual manner and set the skis outside to allow the wax
to freeze. Then, while outside, put a hard wax like Blue or Green over
the klister. If you have a delicate touch you can carefully cork the hard
wax without getting it thoroughly mixed in with the klister. Then the
hard wax will carry you through the powder snow and the klister will
work for you in the granular sections of the track.

The expert waxer will know just how hard to cork the wax and just
how much of the klister to "pull through." Success depends on several
factors, such as the condition of the track, the state of the newer powder
snow, the temperature trends, etc.

The general rule for combining klister and hard wax is this: If the
track dictates using a particular kind of klister and it begins to snow,
or there is some loose snow blowing around, use the appropriate klister
for the granular snow, freeze it, then cover it with the appropriate hard
wax for the powder.

Klister used this way provides a cushion for the granular snow crystals
to indent. The cushion idea comes next.

### Cushion Waxing

Anytime you use hard wax over klister you are applying the cushion
theory. Snow crystals that might not normally indent the hard wax
enough to provide purchase will indent that cushion of klister and provide
hold.

Many skiers have modified cushion waxing to the extent of using only
hard waxes, and the new fiberglass skis, being rather stiff, seem to be
well suited for this type of treatment. Imagine a powder-snow day, warming
in the sun and staying fairly cool in the woods and on the north slopes.
By using a cushion like Hard Red and covering it with something like
Special Blue Hard you avoid the risk of icing in the colder snow, yet
you have that cushion for the soft stuff in the sun.

## HOW TO CHOOSE A WAX

The easiest way to begin waxing is by using a two-wax system. When
the weather and the snow are cold you use the cold snow wax. When it
warms up, use the warmer snow wax.

These waxes have very wide ranges and are often most effective in
widely varying conditions. Racers, who use many different waxes, have
some two-wax systems in their kits just for those days when the waxing
is toughest.

After you learn how to use these two-wax systems you can begin
branching out.

*81. Why? What did you use for wax?*

In the earlier editions of this book I drew up wax charts—but don't look for them now: I've dispensed with them, for several reasons. For one, the usual time-lag between writing something and seeing it printed always seems to give the wax companies time enough to come up with a lot of new waxes. So my charts were slightly outdated before they were published.

Next, the charts and all such may have led skiers to make too much out of wax selection by a brand name. One frequently hears comments to the effect that, "Oh, if you had only used Brand X Blue instead of Brand Y Blue . . ." and so on. Most often, if someone has a problem with waxing it is because he did not apply the wax properly.

Finally, many skiers now possess a higher degree of sophistication about waxing and I don't think they need a chart to tell them when to use Hard Blue, etc.

If you've mastered all the techniques I have described, and if you understand the variables of waxing, you should be in good shape to select a wax.

Read the labels. That's what I do.

Funny thing, but I've outwaxed more coaches than you can imagine by simply following the directions on the wax tins. Most foreign companies have full-time waxing experts who are continually testing their products. These fellows really know their stuff and the only problem for us in North America is that sometimes something will get lost in a faulty translation on the tube. I recall one brand which described the snow conditions for three different klisters in the same way. That wasn't much help, but we knew the klisters were color-keyed (page 101) with other companies' waxes and were able to go on from there.

## SOME GOOD RULES OF THUMB

### Learn How to Use One Brand of Wax Thoroughly Before Branching Out to Another Line

There are several good brands of waxes on the North American market these days and I dare say the vast majority of skiers could get along famously using just one of them.

Learning about one wax includes the study of the basic variables in

---

**WHICH WAX WORKS BEST?**

Lennart Strand, a Swedish ski coach who has been working with the U.S. Team for several years, and I are two people who believe in trying to keep things simple, with emphasis placed on the basics. After our tour with the Team at the Sarajevo Olympic Games in 1984 I wrote Lennart this little note, just to remind him of a joke we had shared during the Games.

Dear Lennart,

I went skiing with my wife the other day and as usual, we waxed our own skis the way we wanted to. I thought I would try a combination that has gained popularity with some of our top racers. I used a thin coat of Fall Line Green to act as a binder and then layered on two coats each of Swix Special Red and Rex Blue Extra, alternating the coats of course. I ironed the wax, then corked it smooth and set the skis outside to cool. I topped it all off with a coat of Rode Multigrade Blue hard wax.

My wife used straight Swix Extra Blue and her skis were just as good as mine. But she doesn't know as much as I do about waxing. Or do you think that maybe she knows more?

Regards,

John

waxing and of the refinements in application methods as well as the use of combinations. Here's a good example of a combination. During the early days of my waxing career Swix was the dominant wax. At one point the company produced Hard Blue and Hard Red, but no Purple. We often had a need for something like the Purple that was still in the future, so we mixed Blue and Red 50–50 on those occasions. We knew what this combination would do and later, when Swix manufactured Purple, we knew exactly how it too would perform. Now many companies have waxes in between the Blue and the Purple, and between the Purple and the Red, and so on.

## Choosing Between Klister and Hard Wax

Developments in track-setting equipment have caused some changes in waxing approaches. In the old days we Easterners were fairly certain when we had to use klister and that was . . . after every rain or serious thaw. (The Westerners have been spared making decisions on klisters for a long time!) Now we might have granular or klister snow, from all appearances, but be better off with binder and hard wax than with klister, especially on cold days. The track-setters and grooming equipment breaks down and mixes the snow more thoroughly and even though the new-set tracks look rigid or firm, they will crumble slightly and after several skiers have used them there will be some loose snow in them. In addition, the snow itself is not so abrasive as that old-time klister snow.

Now, most good waxers prefer a binder and hard wax combination in these conditions. Straight klister, even the hardest, will ice up in cold conditions. It will get a whitish, glazed look and will not be as effective as when it was first applied. So, if you feel you must use klister it's probably a good idea to rub some hard wax appropriate for the temperature on top of it. This may prolong the life of the klister—before it freezes, or ices.

In warmer weather and granular snow nothing much has changed. The soft klisters like the Reds, Yellows, Oranges, Silvers, etc. still work well alone.

## And Two Helpful Procedures

If you are choosing between two hard waxes, try the harder one—the one that is designated for colder conditions—first. If it slips too much, you can always apply the softer wax over it, even out in the snow and on the spur of the moment, as long as your ski is dry. I carry a piece of terrycloth to wipe moisture off the bottoms in cases like this.

And second: Klisters have pretty wide ranges and it's relatively easy to select one. Don't be afraid to get one that is a bit soft to begin with.

If your first klister selection is too hard, trying to add a softer klister will usually prove difficult, if not impossible. Water and dirt get into the original klister and you are apt to have a mess. In fact, it might be easier to clean up and start over again. On the other hand, if the klister is too soft it may wear off enough so that what you have left will work O.K.

## COLOR-KEYED WAXES

Most brands of waxes are color-keyed. This means that the Hard Blue waxes, for instance, are all made for the same snow conditions. There may be slight differences in the Blues and if you are interested in making two of them perform the same way you'll have to make adjustments in the thickness and length of wax on the kicker strip you use.

The colors follow a definite sequence. For most companies their hard waxes go this way—from hardest to softest for snow conditions, and same sequence from cold to warm for air temperature. Special Green, Green, Blue, Purple, Yellow, Red. The Yellows and Reds are sometimes in different order.

So far, so good. But now the companies have introduced combination waxes to be used in between the Greens and Blues, the Blues and Purples, and so on. In some cases a wax slightly harder than Blue might be called Special Blue, or it might be called Super Blue, or Blue Extra, or probably something else by the time this sentence is published. Don't panic! Go back to rule number one. Learn one brand thoroughly and this is not so difficult. Reading the labels will usually tip you off to a particular wax's hardness.

Some also have a binder wax which usually comes in an orange tin and is called Grundvax. I'll describe its use below.

The klisters are not exactly color-keyed according to temperatures since they overlap a great deal, but in general Red and Yellow are the softer klisters, used for warm conditions; Purple, Blue, and Green are the hardest klisters, used for cold conditions, and Silver ranks somewhere between the two extremes. Naturally, the companies are now producing new klisters which fit in between the old colors or supposedly have other special qualities. I'll make a confession here. *It is* getting hard to keep a lot of them straight. Perhaps the companies will pull up short for a while and begin to educate us with pamphlets describing their waxes' capabilities. Just recently they have been flooding the market with so many new products that their promotion departments couldn't keep pace with the publication of proper information.

There is one more problem caused by the appearance of so many new waxes. Their ranges are becoming narrower and narrower. For instance, one type of Blue hard wax might be prescribed for a temperature range of only a few degrees C. This is good if the snow conditions are consistent and if your thermometer is accurate. For most of us, these are two big ifs and we are better off using a wax with a wider range.

### PARAFFIN FOR THE GROOVE, EDGES, AND TOPS

It's a good idea to try and keep purchase wax out of the grooves where it doesn't give you much extra climb, and in certain situations it could ice more easily than the wax on the running surface of your ski bottoms.

But since it's difficult to keep all the wax out of the grooves you should paraffin them after you finish waxing for climb.

Paraffin the edges and tops of the skis as well. Paraffined edges will make the skis run easier; paraffin on the tops helps protect them from moisture and, more important, keeps snow from building up on them. If you really want to carry some extra snow around as you ski, get hold of a backpack and fill it with snow, because that way the stuff won't interfere with your skis' performance.

## Factors Outside the Waxing Room

If you keep a waxing diary, making note of the snow conditions, air temperatures, and how a given wax worked on a certain day, you may run into a few discrepancies. Under seemingly equivalent conditions you will probably find that the Green you used one day worked a lot better on another day. This could be due to one or more of the conditions I list here. It is the consideration of these that separates the expert waxer from the merely good waxer.

### MOISTURE CONTENT IN THE SNOW

If you pick up some snow and squeeze it in your hand every time you wax, you will begin to notice a difference in moisture content. Given the same temperature, snow on one day might be dry and on another day it might squeeze together more, or have more moisture in it.

The more moisture the snow contains the thicker the coat or the softer the wax you will need.

This snow-squeeze test is quite important when using klisters. Some granular snow that is rather cold will have a lot of moisture in it and then you should have some klister softer than Blue in your mixture—you might add Purple.

### TRACK CONDITION

Let me say right here that all purchase waxes are made to perform optimally in packed snow or packed tracks. You can ski in powder snow or loose snow and get some climb from the wax, but you shouldn't expect much. You see, the theory on wax is this: When you press the ski down firmly into the track the snow crystals indent the wax surface and hold you from slipping back. When you take the pressure off the ski you can

## THE ADVANTAGE OF TRACK-SETTERS

Some of the purists decry the advance in track-setting equipment, but there are some advantages to the track skier when machines can grind up old, hard snow and mix it with any new snow that might have fallen recently. It makes a uniform mix and track conditions are more stable. Wax works better. Waxless skis, properly chosen, work better.

At the 1984 Winter Olympics in Sarajevo the organizers did an excellent job with the tracks. The temperatures did not vary much and conditions did not change during any of the races. This made for very fair races, especially compared to those the year before at the pre-Olympics when they turned into waxing contests. In fact, it was rather humorous at the Olympics. The world's waxing experts were at the ready, studying weather and snow conditions daily, testing wax on various parts of the courses and radioing in information to the central wax hut, eagerly waiting for something different to happen. But it never did. I'll wager that 95 to 100 percent of the racers competing went out with some brand of Blue hard wax—every single day, every single race.

slide it ahead easily. If you don't have a firm snow surface to press the ski wax against, the crystals will not indent the wax.

Look at it this way. Sand makes for wonderful traction on the roads in winter driving conditions. It gets between your tires and the road surface and gives your tires something to grip. But how much grip does sand give when you drive around on a soft sandy beach?

So if the track you're in is soft, or loose, you'll need more kicker. Use a softer wax, or a thicker coat, or a longer kicker, or all three.

If you're skiing in new snow don't expect too much success with any wax. Actually, deep loose snow gives you hold in other ways. And I know a lot of people who would trade such snow for some purchase from wax, any day.

### OLD, TIRED SNOW

In some areas where they have mechanical track-setting equipment, complete with those rototillers which beat up and mix the snow, you run into what I call tired snow. At the World Championships in Oslo in 1982 there was little, if any, new snow during the period preceding the races and for the races themselves. Every day, according to established procedures, the course crews went out and ground up the snow and set new tracks. By the time the last race came around the snow was so tired, the crystals so rounded and smashed, that it could barely stick together, even when compressed. I remember stepping into a "fresh" track, right after the track machine had gone by. I shouted at the snow and it crumbled, right there! (Well, maybe not quite!)

Snow like this will require softer wax than the temperatures otherwise indicate. The reason is obvious: The snow crystals are very rounded and won't stick into hard wax.

### WEATHER FORECAST

You can be better informed about making a waxing decision if you know the weather forecast. What is the trend? If the local forecast calls for warming, take this fact into consideration and wax accordingly. Or, if you're going on a tour, take the next warmest wax along with you. And so on.

### TRAIL EXPOSURE

If your trail is located primarily in the woods, in shady sections, or on the north slopes (the southern slopes in Australia!), you can be sure the snow will be colder than out in the open on a sunny slope. It would probably be a good idea to wax for the colder snow and take your chances with the warm stuff.

### AIR TEMPERATURE VS SNOW TEMPERATURE

There is usually good correlation between the air temperature and the performance of the wax assigned for that temperature. For instance, if it's somewhere in the range of $-3°$ to $-8°$ C (roughly 26° to 18° F) outside and you have powder snow, most Hard Blue waxes will work well. But you might go out on Blue in conditions like this someday with a friend only to have him tell you he is on Hard Green wax and really enjoying it—good purchase, good glide, the whole works. Chances are the snow temperature is considerably colder than the air temperature, thus accounting for the difference in wax performance.

If you know two things about snow temperatures it will help you wax. First, snow temperature is almost always colder than air temperature; this should be obvious on days when the air temperature is above freezing, because if snow gets above freezing it turns to water. Second, snow temperatures rise more slowly than air temperatures do.

In the case above, the "Blue wax" day was probably preceded by some colder weather which helped to make the snow cold, and it was still cold even though the air temperatures had warmed.

Cold temperatures form more small, very sharp ice crystals, or snow-flakes if you want to call them that. Sharp crystals will more easily indent hard wax than the softer, more rounded crystals that make up warmer snow. So when I'm serious about waxing I whip out two ther-mometers, one for the air temp and one for the snow temp. If the air is $-5°$ C (23° F) and the snow is $-10°$ C (14° F) I would start testing Green, or even Special Green, and then work up from there, knowing I could easily add a softer wax if it was needed.

## CLEANING SKIS

Sooner or later you will have to clean your skis. Sooner, no doubt, if you use waxable skis. You can get a lot of conflicting advice on cleaning procedures if you look around enough. I recall the U.S. Team was touting some chemical solvent a few years back—this one really did the job and was very popular until some report mentioned the possibility that it was a cancer-causing agent.

Methods for cleaning skis vary, but the most important distinction should be made between waxless and waxable skis.

With waxable skis you can use almost any proven method. I prefer to stay away from chemicals and scrape as much wax as possible off my skis, then use a torch and rag to finish up. The wax is usually easier to scrape off when it's cold.

Wax companies have several good wax removers and these can be used with success. I can't bear the cost of the removers, and besides, I kind of like the sticky fingers that come from using heat and rags.

I have a favorite method for taking off hard wax which is this: I come in and find some leftover pieces of glider wax and melt them over the

---

**WAX BOX INGREDIENTS**

To keep your waxes in good condition and handy, sooner or later you'll need a wax box. I recommend the kind of sturdy metal box used for tools or fishing tackle; size and complexity of compartments depend on how serious you are about waxing. I'm not sold on cloth bags much: They're hard to clean, easy to puncture, and often wear out.

In the box you'll have your favorite waxes and a small slab of paraffin, then these things: Screwdriver and pliers. A paintbrush, and a couple of corks—one for very hard and one for softer waxes—since you shouldn't use the same cork for both. A tool for making Hairies. Spare screws for your bindings and spare screws or nails for your heelplates. Steel wool, sandpaper, and some clean rags. A scraper for the ski bottoms and one for the groove, and a file to sharpen the scraper. Some wire. Adhesive tape or straps for tying your skis together. Matches in a moisture-proof metal container. Handcleaner or Vaseline. Wax solvent. A thermometer or two, for testing air and snow temperatures. If your box is big enough, a discarded but workable flatiron whose temperature settings you can rely on; a small butane torch. A wax chart—if you can still find one these days—for the brand of waxes you prefer (mount it on a stiff card and cover it with clear plastic wrap used for food). And your small waxing diary, and a pencil.

entire length of the ski, then iron everything together. This ironing—I believe—helps improve the running surface of the ski, waxes over any dry spots, and builds up a layer of wax which I can easily scrape off after it cools. I scrape harder under the foot in order to leave bare the kicker zone, but leave enough glider wax on tips and tails for my next outing.

Some skis' bottoms are damaged by the use of heat from a torch or an iron. For instance, if you use enough heat you can easily round the edges of the designs on waxless skis, the very designs that are there to give you grip. Some other waxless skis, including some you can wax, have bottoms which react adversely to heat and the only thing you can use here is a solvent. But, all waxless skis, even your own Hairies, will pick up dirt or klister from a track, and will eventually need cleaning. And, in general, solvents are the most foolproof to use.

## THUMBNAIL WAXING SUMMARY

Learn one brand of wax thoroughly before turning to another. Most tourskiers can enjoy x-c without investing in the racers' repertory of waxes anyway.

Begin waxing with a warm, dry ski in a warm room.

Choose a wax by (a) using the outside air temperature as a guide, then (b) paying attention to the range/instructions printed on each wax container's label.

Smooth the wax well, and allow it to cool outside before using your skis.

Don't be afraid to experiment. Don't be bound by such statements as "You can never put a harder wax over a softer wax": Of course you can.

Keep an account of your waxing results, in your head or, better, in a little diary-notebook tucked in your box. The expert is the waxer who remembers combinations that succeeded in oddball conditions.

# 8

# Conditioning

A TEMPTING APPROACH TO conditioning is to tell you that I can't possibly cover all aspects here and refer you to some more specialized texts, listed in the back of the book. Well, the books are listed but I also want to tell you how I see this training or conditioning business as it applies to you.

The best recommendation I can make is this: You should approach your off-season physical activities with the same effort or intensity you plan to use when you go skiing. If you think that touring is so easy that you need no prior conditioning I'm afraid you will find yourself sadly mistaken. You can't lead a very sedentary life and then just start skiing.

**82.** *When snow comes late in the East many eager skiers take to their ice skates.*

Or, at the other end of the spectrum, if you think you will perform well in your local Citrace with no training, you're in for another shocker. You can't fool your body. If you jump into some new physical activity all of a sudden and with moderate effort, you will suffer some consequences, even if it's only a few stiff muscles.

Conditioning, or training, usually implies participation in some future activity. People who practice, or condition themselves for their activity are the ones who execute it most successfully.

## THE THREE GROUPS OF TOURSKIERS

Most tourskiers fall into one of three groups. I'll call the first one the active, outdoors-type bunch. People in this group have a love for the out-of-doors. They often do some kind of physical work—like mowing the lawn—taking walks or hikes, occasionally doing backpacking trips, river trips, or bike tours. Or, at least they would like to do these things. The main purpose of these outings is to enjoy life or maintain this kind of lifestyle. Conditioning is not a primary concern. In fact, they sometimes feel miffed if you even suggest they are in effect conditioning themselves. They really are! But they don't like to think of it that way. However, they aren't going to have too much trouble going out for a nice tour when the snow comes in the winter.

I belong to this group, except that I admit to training once in a while. I don't train enough to belong to the second group.

This second group of people actually plan their exercise and may get addicted to it, or at least count on it as an enjoyable routine. Their exercise may be something as simple as walking or jogging around a few blocks in town several days a week. It might be something more demanding like running or biking a fair distance several times a week. These people do it because it makes them feel good and they sometimes can be tempted to enter a little road race, bike race, or even a ski touring race. But they are not going to worry too much about a serious, more scientific approach to conditioning.

The third group of people are more eager to train or build themselves up, and want to improve their times and performances in whatever events they enter. They usually seek out coaching and training advice and have a program laid out which they try to follow conscientiously. If you belong to this group I have a few hints for you in this chapter. I must also refer you to the more complete texts listed in the Reference section.

Now that I have tried to categorize most of you, I feel a bit like Garrison Keillor when he gets into one of his monologues and asks, "How am I going to get out of this one?" But it's easy. I'm going to strike off and write about conditioning and ask you to pick and choose whatever you

**83. and 84.** *Hill striding with poles (83) and without poles (84).*

want. You see, the crossovers between the groups are increasing in number and the possibilities for conditioning are so numerous and so rich it would be a shame to feel restricted by such nonsense as having someone tell you that biking is not good training, especially as fall approaches, or that hiking isn't specific enough to skiing. More and more skiers don't hesitate to do what they want, even if their exercise habits appear to be inconsistent from week to week, or year to year. It's O.K. And maybe it works.

## MAJOR TRAINING NOTIONS

There are a few basic tenets to any good conditioning program and the ones I list here may raise a few eyebrows, particularly because there is not a big emphasis on practicing the specific event, in this case, cross-country skiing.

### Confidence and Enjoyment

The primary ingredient for conditioning yourself may be a love of exercise, whether it's in a gym in the city, or outdoors in the countryside. I'm one who believes that our bodies were designed for a fair amount of physical activity. Isn't that how our ancestors survived? We aren't so far removed from the primates . . . yet . . . and that feeling of well-being that comes after exercise isn't matched by anything I know of. At any rate, if you don't enjoy your exercise the chances are good that you won't continue with it. So try to get into something that is pleasurable for you.

---

**SCANDINAVIANS AND TRAINING**

Because of their success in international skiing competition we always assume that the Scandinavian countries have bullet-proof training programs. We think . . . if we could only copy them perhaps we would hit the top. But during the 1984 season, including the Olympic Games, the top female Swedish racer, Lillemor Marie Risby, and the top male Norwegian racer, Lars-Erik Eriksen, were not part of their national programs. Eriksen has had several difficulties with the brass in Norway and at one point was practically banned from the team, its training camps, all coaching advice, etc. Risby simply wanted to continue her education, therefore was dropped from the Swedish team and received no financial support. They both trained on their own and it worked well. You should feel the same way about any program you pursue. There's more than one way to skin a cat.

---

I've seen lots of athletes who have lacked confidence in their training programs. Often someone else who is following the same program, but with confidence, comes along and performs better.

There are so many different ways to condition yourself that it would be impossible for an exercise physiologist to begin to list them all. Doctors and scientists are learning new approaches all the time. You should feel confident about your program and this may require some careful planning or help from someone who is qualified. And you can measure your progress too. (I'll say more about this in the section on Aids, page 117.)

## Harder Day, Easier Day

Day on, day off, is an old approach to training. What it means is that on one day you exercise harder than average and on the other day you take it easier than your average. Done correctly this simple system gives your body a chance to rest, or recover, no matter what level of exercise you may be working at.

This is so basic and so important that it amazes me when people don't follow this regimen. Maybe it's too easy to figure out. For example, if you want to jog three miles every day, change it around so that one day you jog three and one-half miles, and the next day, two and one-half. You'll get your six miles in every two days this way.

I know some skiers who bike to work during the off-season and even though the distance is constant this system is used. They bike hard one day and much less hard the next. Same thing.

## Regularity

If you exercise on a regular basis you will be successful with your program ... and this doesn't mean you have to go out daily. Some people can maintain their level of conditioning by exercising 15–20 minutes a day, three times a week. Chances are they cannot improve their conditioning too much with this program, but they can do a good job of keeping an even keel.

More typical programs might include something done regularly during the working days of the week and then some special events on the weekends.

## Progress

In order to improve your fitness you have to build an element of progression into your program. You can do this in terms of the time spent exercising, or in terms of the intensity with which you exercise, or—if you are really serious about competition—in both these areas.

If you are beginning a program you might start out with your basic

## TWO TRAINING SCHEDULES

Here are two training programs from opposite ends of the spectrum. Each one is set up for the off-snow season, at least measured in the northern climes. The first is for someone beginning an exercise program and the second is one prescribed for a serious college ski racer.

## BEGINNING SCHEDULE

*May:* Walk one mile 2x a week, one-half mile 2x a week. If this seems too easy after two weeks, pick up the pace.

*June:* Walk one mile 2x a week, one-half mile 2x a week, at an increased pace. Take part in some weekend physical activity, such as hiking.

*July:* Walk one and one-half miles 2x a week, one mile 2x a week. If this seems too easy after two weeks, intersperse walking with easy jogging.

*August:* Walk one and one-half miles 2x a week at a good pace. Jog one mile 2x a week. Don't worry if you can't finish the jog—walk it in. Take some easy weekend exercise, such as hiking.

*September:* Jog/walk 2 miles 2x a week. Jog/walk one mile 2x a week. Take weekend hike or do some physical activity.

*October:* Jog/walk two and one-half miles a week. Jog/walk one and one-half miles a week. Take a weekend hike.

## COLLEGE RACER'S SCHEDULE

*May:*      15 ten-second hill sprints 3x a week
            upper body strength work 3x a week, leg strength 2x a week
            2–3 hour hike once a week
            roller ski 3x a week
            run 3x a week
                                      TOTAL 10 hours a week

*June:*     Same as May, TOTAL 11 hours a week
*July:*     Same as June, TOTAL 12 hours a week
*August:*   Same as July, TOTAL 13 hours a week
*September:* Same as August, with following changes or additions:
            Hike once 3–4 hours
            Intervals 2x a week
            Run 2x a week
            Race pace once a week
                                      TOTAL 14 hours a week
*October:*  Same as September except running 3x a week
                                      TOTAL 15 hours a week

walk, doing it four to five times a week and going just a mile. After a couple of weeks you could increase the distance to a mile and one-half. Do this for another week, or two. Increase it again. And so on. About the time you begin to feel frisky, or think your routine is too easy, or that it is going to take too much time if you add another mile, pull back a bit on the distance and increase your intensity. Walk much faster. Or begin to jog for short distances.

All programs that have progress built into them work like this. The key factor is progressing slowly and listening to your body. If you begin to get tired you have probably tried to take too big an increase. You should hold back until you feel more comfortable. Too many athletes get impatient with a rather deliberate program and go busting off, only to end up tired, injured, or feeling a bit down. Don't push it too fast.

## Specificity

Doing exercise specific to your activity is always helpful. In cross-country skiing the best way to condition yourself is to go cross-country skiing. (Some people get paid for saying things like this!) The next best thing is roller-skiing. After that, pulling on armbands, ice-skating, roller-skating, using those road skates designed for hockey players, using a roller-board, and any other exercises which incorporate skiing motions are good.

But don't get hung up on doing these off-season exercises. You will survive without them. There is always the possibility of getting rather tired or bored with specificity exercises so that when snow comes you don't get that thrill of skiing. Everything is too routine.

A different kind of specificity applies to the total amount of muscle mass you use doing your exercise. Since skiing involves the use of most of your body's muscles it's good to train this way too. For instance, strengthening one arm on a machine isn't going to give your cardiovascular system the benefits that rowing will.

## Rest

The day on, day off approach is designed mainly for recovery. Sometimes you get into a program and begin to stall out. You don't look forward to your routine. Your muscles feel tired, or tight walking up a flight of stairs. When this happens it's time for rest. This can take different forms. Straight rest would involve no exercise and this might be indicated. However, a change of activity for a few days might also accomplish the same thing.

It's best to be conservative and take plenty of rest. Most athletes schedule a rest day once a week, just for openers. It's better to rest too much than too little.

## Stretches

I have listed stretches here to attract your attention because they are NOT a major component in a conditioning program for cross-country skiing. Some magazine articles are a bit misleading when they publish those "Get Fit for Skiing" articles and tout pictures of people in underwear doing stretches.

Stretches can be valuable if done before and after some of your more strenuous training stints, ones which may focus on your major muscle groups. For instance, you have to get your legs in shape and stretches alone won't do this. Stretches won't help your cardiovascular system either. I advise athletes to do stretches but not to count them as part of the hours per week they are targeted for.

## The Cardiovascular System

Most of the training for x-c skiing is concentrated on improving the cardiovascular system—that is, developing the ability to pump or deliver oxygen in the blood to all parts of the body. There is always debate over the most efficient way to train your system and if you read far enough you can find almost any approach you like. Running remains the most popular and will continue to be so. It's right at hand, involves your legs, and you can work at a whole range of intensities. Be sure to work on your cv system if you want to get in shape.

# THE COMPONENTS

Every well-designed program has elements from the following areas, or conditioning groups: distance training for endurance, interval training, speed and tempo training, strength training, and technique and coordination training. Good racers include all of these in their programs and the wiser ones concentrate on their weaknesses during the off-season. If you are low-key about your conditioning you would be best off sticking to distance training and working on your technique.

## Distance (Endurance) Training

This is just what it says: a long workout that's designed to build endurance in the athlete.

Most physiologists, coaches and trainers feel that distance training is the most important aspect of anyone's program.

Running, jogging, biking, hiking in rugged terrain or with a pack, canoeing, kayaking, rather heavy work like logging or pick-and-shovel jobs—all these qualify as methods of endurance training. Another rough

**85.** *Vintage picture. U.S. Ski Team on its hike of the Long Trail in Vermont, 1968.*

guide is this: Your heartbeat should average right around 120 per minute, counting spurts and lags, during these workouts.

Furthermore, it probably makes sense to take it easier for at least one day between good (for "good," read "hard") distance days. The body can use the respite to recover.

### Interval Training

Interval training is repeated exercises broken up by "rest" periods.

The most common type of interval training is running. Athletes run a prescribed distance at a fixed speed, return to the start and rest, or jog a bit until they are rested, and run again. There are lots of variables here—the number of intervals you do, the distance you run, the speed with which you run, and the amount of time you rest. For instance, the number of repetitions might vary from 5 to 50, the distance from 50 yards to several hundred yards, the speed at which you run from half-effort to all-out, and the degree of rest from partial to fairly complete.

Here are a couple of rough guides to help you with your interval training.

Rest after each set until your heart rate goes down to 120 per minute (I'm assuming you worked hard enough to get it up over 120). Get a rough approximation of the recovery time you need to get your pulse back down. Continue with the exercises until your recovery time is quite a bit longer than it was at first, or until you feel tired or stiff doing your workout. If doing an interval workout seems to take too long—i.e., that it takes too long to get tired or to slow down your recovery rate—then you can work harder or longer at your particular exercise. For instance, you might be running 60-yard intervals and find it takes a long time to get the effect of having had a workout. So jump the distance to 80 to 100 yards and run faster.

One theory behind interval training is that while you are waiting for your heart rate to return to 120 you are actually conditioning your cardiovascular system because of the stress it is under. Herein lies the beauty of interval training. During a period of 20 minutes of interval training, you might actually be resting or jogging, while your recovery takes place, for 12 to 14 minutes. In other words, your leg muscles, etc., are not being called upon to perform under stress for more than 6 to 8 minutes.

Proponents of the interval-training method claim that in addition to being a good conditioner for the cardiovascular system, it at the same time improves your ability to recover from vigorous exercise.

You can do lots of things for interval training. The more common approaches are running, biking, swimming, or rowing rather vigorously for short periods of time. But, during a distance workout, you could incorporate some interval training by going fast for a stretch and then taking it easy (like jogging while running, coasting while biking or skiing, etc.) for a while until your recovery was complete.

## Speed/Tempo Training

This kind of training is interpreted two ways. Generally, tempo training means training at racing speed, for whatever event you are working for. Speed training can mean this also; but it is used by some to mean sprint, or top-speed, training. I shall use it as meaning sprinting or going all-out.

### TEMPO TRAINING

Tempo training is used to condition yourself for performing at racing speeds. It is so similar to interval training that often the two kinds of workouts are lumped together. Sometimes tempo training takes place for periods of time equal to ⅓ to ⅔ of the time required to run the event you're training for.

### SPEED TRAINING

Speed training is used to train the body to be able to perform faster.

With speed training, by my definition, you go all-out for a rather short period of time, then take a good rest by waiting until the pulse is well under 120 per minute, and repeat.

## Strength Training

Most of the recent advances and changes in the training program of top athletes have occurred in their strength-training program. Almost every world class athlete does some kind of strength training these days.

If you have access to some of the more sophisticated equipment like Universal Gyms and the Nautilus machines, you can work out a very good program for yourself. But be sure to do it with the advice of someone competent in this area. There's no sense in straining or injuring yourself through ignorance.

I count three kinds of physical strength. One is gained by weight-lifting, which is especially good for those muscles involved in lifting weights—and these are not always the same ones that you need in skiing.

Another kind of strength is gained by doing special exercises related to the skiing motions, like pulling on tough elastic ropes or similar devices that offer resistance when you pull. (A couple of decades ago we were using old bicycle innertubes for such exercise; they became known as "Putney armbands.")

The third kind of strength training is that which develops what I call overall coordinated body strength. When you get out there skiing you have to put it all together. The fellow who can press a lot of weight or pull the armbands until the cows come home is not necessarily going to be able to combine all his movements into a strong, coordinated effort on the ski track. Certain kinds of exercises like rock-climbing and gymnastics are very good for this coordinated strength.

Other hard work like shoveling, digging ditches (without a backhoe), cutting wood with an axe, chain-saw (these are O.K.) or cross-cut, all qualify. Hiking with heavy packs is good.

## AIDS

Having discussed the basics and some of the components for a conditioning program, it's a good time to list a few aids which can be valuable.

### The Log

All serious skiers keep a training journal and it's easy to do. You don't have to spend much time on this and the payback is very high.

Assuming you have an overall plan you can list it early on in your log and then as the months go by, check back to see if you are on course.

By recording your efforts, times for a workout, or your overall feeling, you have something to compare with later on. You might think you are not making any progress and then look back into your log and find it

**86–88.** *Roller boards and armband devices are good for strengthening the upper body.*

**89.** *Training sculls, or ocean sculls as these pictured offer good chances for exercise.*

took you quite a bit longer to do a certain workout just a few months ago. This is bound to give you a boost.

In the big time, coaches and physiologists make a habit of studying athletes' training logs in an effort to discover why a certain effect took place. With no record, everyone is participating in guesswork.

## Social Aspects

The social aspects of training are so important that I almost included them under major categories above, but then I thought I would never hear the end of that classification.

If you're a loner you don't need this socializing that takes place during workouts. But pity those of us who need it, who indeed, count on it to help carry us along. I love it and know I wouldn't do half as much if it weren't for the camaraderie that comes with training.

## The Diet

Most Americans have access to plenty of good food and barely a week goes by without some reference in the news to proper diet. All the recommended diets I have read about pertain to cross-country skiers as well. There is just one thing to add: If you exercise a lot and need more calories, take up the slack by increasing the amounts of carbohydrates you eat. And no, you won't get fat.

119

In fact, exercising is the best way to lose weight. In most situations your caloric demands do not increase enough to keep pace with the body's energy requirements.

### PR Monitors

There are a lot of pulse rate monitors on the market now and we will see more and more sophisticated ones coming out. The best way to control the level of intensity while exercising is by using your heart rate as a guide. Some monitors have upper and lower settings with beepers that go off when you exceed these limits. So, if you wanted to run along at an effort that produced a pulse rate between 120 and 140 all you'd have to do would be adjust the monitor, get warmed up, run a bit to bring your pulse rate up, turn on the machine, and listen.

### The Big Occasion

An element of anticipation and excitement can be added to any program by scheduling something out-of-the-ordinary. It could be a destination hike with friends to some far-off place, entering a road race or a bike time trial, taking a long row, and so on. A commitment like this provides a wonderful focus for many people. To say nothing of the war stories that you can swap after the event.

## MEDICAL ASPECTS

More and more doctors ski cross-country these days. Those fellows have discovered the joys and benefits of the sport. The spin-off benefit for you is that your chances of dealing with a skiing doctor have increased. The ones who have skied cross-country are probably in the best position to advise you on any x-c medical questions.

### A Check-up

If you are going to embark on a reasonably vigorous program you should get a check-up from your doctor. Outline to him your plans and get his O.K. If you run into problems along the way your doctor can probably advise you as well.

### Sickness

Once again, check with your doctor if you get sick and have some questions about what to do. If it will save you an office call I'll tell you now that there is no such thing as running off a cold. Forget it. Rest until it goes

**90. and 91.** *Start of the Tour of the Valley bike race in Putney, Vermont.*

**92–94.** *This cast for a broken leg was specially fitted to allow biking and even roller skiing.*

away, or until you begin to feel better, then proceed slowly. Don't ever take a chance on getting further run down when you are sick. By training when you are sick you could easily complicate matters.

## Bone and Joint Injuries

I've had my share of problems with bones and joints and can report that often there is some exercise you can do during your convalescence period. The orthopedic specialists are the ones to give prescriptions here and many of them will assist you in order to help your recuperation. I've biked with a cast on a broken ankle. No problem. Skiers can roller-ski with a cast on for a lower leg break. People break wrists, hands, fingers, and get special casts which permit them to hold a pole and ski. After knee operations, swimming or beginning to walk while partially submerged in water is often helpful and possible.

The point is not to give up. There's probably something you can do and you will be very thankful for the opportunity.

# ROLLER-SKIING

Skiers in our area have been at roller-skiing for many years, dating from the mid '60s. We've seen the models change time after time and the pattern has been a familiar one. Some of the first roller skis were real klunkers and I wonder how we managed them at all. Then a few companies came in with some rather makeshift equipment that didn't work well or last long, and now—due to increasing popularity—several companies are beginning to vie for leadership in the production of roller skis.

The main virtue of roller-skiing is that it is very much like snow skiing. The movements are exactly the same although perhaps not so quick as on snow. Roller-skiing is an excellent way to train, to practice technique, and to get around on the roads. It's thrilling—sometimes a bit too thrilling!—and no doubt will continue to increase in popularity.

### SOME DRAWBACKS TO ROLLER-SKIING

There are several drawbacks to roller-skiing and with its increased use by tourskiers I quickly point them out:

1. If you are not a good snow skier you may have trouble with the roller skis and fall. When you fall it's awfully tough landing on the pavement.
2. Road and highway traffic is always a threat to pedestrians, so if you go out of control on roller skis the results could be very serious.

**95.** *Roller skiing above I–91 in Vermont.*

    **3.** Due to the danger, many areas, and some countries, are outlawing the use of roller skis on public highways. You might get a pair of skis and find you couldn't use them in your area anymore, so inquire.

It follows that when you begin roller-skiing you should select a road that is not heavily traveled.

If the downhills are at all steep you are well advised to take your skis off and walk rather than risking a fall or collision.

Practice just a few minutes a day for several outings until you gain some skill and balance. Then you can take longer trips.

### THE FUTURE OF ROLLER-SKIING

Some roller skis are designed for use on dirt roads or smooth terrain like athletic fields and golf courses. These take the skiers off the highways and in general offer a more pleasant outing.

The Germans have designed special tracks which can be laid out on gentle terrain and used for roller-skiing. This very specialized approach may be the best way to go. It eliminates many of the hazards and skiers don't have to share space with cars, golfers, soccer players, etc.

# 9

# Where to Find It

IN THE EARLY DAYS of x-c skiing, when anyone who skied was considered some sort of pioneer, skiing was to be had almost anywhere there was snow. At least that's what many claimed. Tracks were seen in what seemed to be the oddest places—because the sport was new and not as organized as it is today. Then x-c'ers felt the freedom that went with the sport and many developed the attitude that skiing was free, too. Well, it still is free in many places but today, the majority of skiers use ski-touring centers. That's where it's happening. If you haven't tried

**96.** *During the famous blizzard of '78 many Boston area residents found that skiing to market was the only way to go.*

**97.** *Schoolteacher starts to school during the famous Eastern blizzard of March '84.*

them, give 'em a break. They are trying to promote the sport and they need help.

Consider the work and the facilities that are necessary to run an area. First, they need some property and permission to use it. A main hut or shop would be a high priority, as well as a parking lot. The trails need marking, clearing, leveling, grooming (especially in low snowfall areas), and packing on a regular basis. A small snowmobile, the type which many skiing schools use for their programs, costs in excess of $5000 at this writing, and a small x-c area would be hard pressed to get by using just one machine like this.

Then suppose everything is set up for the season and there is no snow, or at best, marginal snow conditions. Snowmaking, you ask? How many areas can afford this? And have you considered the logistics in snowing even a 3 km track around the countryside?

I know it still bothers some skiers to think about paying trail fees to go skiing, but a few dollars for all this preparation is a bargain. If you don't believe it, try working on the management end of the area someday.

Many people have never skied out of tracks and probably have no knowledge of this experience. Or have no desire to try it. The problem is, I don't have to tell you trackless skiers about the joys of. You know all about it. You know about tracks, too, most likely. And if I encourage all the track skiers to go exploring off on their own there could be some problems with safety. People still get lost skiing. Unfortunately, some perish every year. So I encourage beginners to go to ski areas that specialize in x-c and then, after they feel strong and competent, to try some off-track skiing. As starters, I have written in Chapter 10 about going out for the day and about precautions that should be observed. This approach or list of precautions is not meant to be exhaustive but certainly suggestive.

## SKI TOURING CENTERS

Meanwhile I'll talk about ski-touring centers and what to look for at one.

There are four criteria that should be considered in selecting an area that specializes in x-c. These are not listed in order of importance because I'm sure they vary with different individuals.

### Instruction

If you don't believe in instruction, that's O.K. You don't have to take it and can do it your own way. But there are thousands of certified ski-touring instructors in the United States alone. Most of these teachers belong to professional organizations that are continually studying the best methods of instruction, among other things. They care, they want to help you to become a happy x-c'er. You might give them a try some day.

As for the point on teaching expert technique—well, there are techniques and there are techniques. I think that what we consider racing technique will become accepted as expert touring technique and that other touring techniques will differ mainly in the degree of effort expended. My own definition of expert touring technique is that which is the most efficient way to ski. It's the technique where you get the most for your effort. It's the optimum way to ski. That's the way I try to ski, even when I'm "racing."

### Trail Systems

A good area should have a trail system complete with markings, and a map showing difficult trails, vertical climbs and drops, etc. The trail-sweep at the end of the day is an important consideration. No matter what, a skier can sometimes get lost or have equipment trouble, and if he is out late in the afternoon the trail-sweep will pick him up. In my conversations with area managers they remark that the trail-sweep is worthwhile even if only one straggler is picked up all season.

> **WOODFORD STATE PARK**
>
> Living in southern Vermont we often get impatient for snow in November and start phoning our friends up north or looking to the higher elevations. Several years ago we discovered a little place called Woodford State Park which sits on a plateau at the western edge of the Green Mountains about 35 miles from my home. The state maintains picnic sites and lean-tos here during the summer months and then closes it during the fall. But that doesn't stop it from getting all sorts of early snow. One year skiing began there in late October and went right through until late April when people got tired of it.
>
> Even though the park is located near to lots of other places in this small state it picks up snow when no other site does. The weather there is something of a meteorological wonder. So many skiers were using the area that their parked cars began clogging the highway that runs right by and the state built a parking lot across the road for them. The state police give gentle reminders now—I believe they're called tickets—that skiers should use the parking place and not park on the side of the road.
>
> Lots of localities have their Woodfords and it's only a matter of searching them out, or listening to a few of the natives talk about the early snowfalls. It's always difficult to believe someone who lives at a higher location describe the snow "in the backyard" but there's more to it than exaggeration.

If the area has double-tracks it's a lot of fun to go skiing side-by-side with a friend. It's just like jogging together and as long as neither one of you has to work so hard that you huff and puff, you can have a pleasant conversation.

## Rentals (and Waxing)

You don't have to rely solely on the x-c area for rental service but most places are set up for it, and the chances are that you will have better luck if you go with them all the way. You know how it is when you take your new GM car to a Ford dealership for servicing. . . .

In any case, you shouldn't have to get hung up on waxing. If you use the waxless skis you are all set, at least temporarily. If the place rents you skis, it obviously has wax, benches, and all the other facilities for waxing, and you can let them do it for you.

## Non-Skiing, Social Aspects

There is no question that services which are not directly related to skiing are becoming more and more important. I'm talking about the food service, a place to lounge and brownbag it or socialize, overnight facilities, entertainment, and all that. Many skiers are coming from outside the snowbelt and they need a place to stay if they take a weekend to go x-c skiing. And this is just the beginning. I think the most successful x-c areas are going to be the ones that provide something else which is unusual, or unique, in addition to all the skiing-related services like tracks, instruction, ski shops, and rentals. So look for it and don't be surprised.

### TRACKS VS NO TRACKS

Before I discuss the value of tracks I want to mention the general difference between touring terrain in the eastern part of North America and in the West. Snow in the East is likely to be harder and, further, terrain in our mountains is choppier—more rugged and with more undergrowth— than prevails in, say high country in the West. Like all generalities, this one of course has plenty of exceptions, but it does account for a good deal of the controversy on this side of the Atlantic over the pleasures of packed trails with tracks as opposed to no packing and no tracks.

Tourskiers of long standing always remember with pleasure some of their super days out on the snow. And depending on what section of the country they are from they will vouch for track skiing or just plain open skiing. I've been lucky enough to do plenty of both and I will admit that going out in the right conditions and skiing anywhere without having to follow a track is unbeatable. Since x-c tracks usually provide the best and most available skiing in my area, however, I follow them for 90 percent of my skiing.

The advantages and disadvantages of both kinds of skiing are pretty obvious. It may turn out that if you are in trackless ski country you will yearn for tracks and if you're in my area where tracks abound you will wait for the day when conditions permit some free skiing.

It's pretty clear that beginners can learn to ski much easier on a packed trail that has tracks set in it. The tracks help stabilize the skis, and in fact do much to direct the skis. To repeat the obvious, this is one of the advantages of a touring center. You can expect to find tracks here.

In general, tracks provide more uniform snow conditions and are faster. If you ski in unbroken snow you are apt to push warmer, wetter surface snow into contact with drier snow underneath, with the result that your skis ice up. You only have to compare skiing in a track to know that the track is faster. Many is the time I've leaped out of the track on a downhill to get into some unbroken stuff and slow down.

Finally, tracks *always* go somewhere and having them usually means you have something to follow to keep from getting lost. (Although I recall following tracks around the top of a mountain in Germany for an hour or two and not being able to find my way back to the parking lot. Finally, an obliging fellow led me there.) If you are out on your own and if your tracks disappear, because of a snowfall, darkness, or even extreme melting, you have a better chance of getting lost.

## Club Possibilities

With so many x-c skiers around these days it's only a matter of time before some of them group together and form clubs so they can enjoy the sport in their own way. All that's needed to begin with is some land in snow-country that is good for touring. If the club or a club member owns the land that's fine. If the club arranges for permission to use the property that's good, too. From this point, the projects can begin—building of an overnight lodge, cutting trails, fund-raising events for equipment, membership drives, arranging for movies, instruction, and so on. Many clubs arrange special events during the season—as a focus. For example, the Nordic Ski Club of Anchorage, Alaska, rents a train to get its members to the site of one of its annual tours. Membership being around 2800 at this writing, a caravan of chartered buses wouldn't be so much fun, and riding in private vehicles could get a bit cramped.

### THEIR POTENTIAL FOR SPORT AND CONSERVATION

For the ultimate in trail systems we could follow the example of Norway. There they have been at it a long time, and it shows: Skiers can go for hundreds of kilometers with assurance of being on marked terrain and finding overnight accommodations in the chain of cabins run by the Norwegian Ski Federation.

We have the same potential here in North America, and I'm confident that sometime soon we'll have the opportunity to ski 60–80 kilometers on a trip in one day, or take tours lasting several days; and neither possibility will be beyond the scope of a competent skier who's been active in a good progressive club.

Another benefit that clubs can offer is to foster x-c among young people who aren't exposed to the sport in school or college. Further, they can provide a base for x-c among those who, although they have had it in their curriculum, might otherwise give it up after graduation.

And, last, there's no question that more effort must be made to control use of public lands better, and to save wilderness areas. X-C clubs can play a big role in such conservation measures, and right on the local level, as well as banded together for broader effectiveness.

## Citizen Races

Just as marathons for footrunners are increasing in number, so are marathons, or Citraces, for cross-country skiers.

The most notable races in the States, at this writing, are the ones that comprise the Great American Ski Chase. This is a series of about eight races (depending on the year) spread throughout the snowbelt and throughout the winter. The races average from 50–60 km in length and, in one instance, at Bemidjii, Minnesota, there are races on two consecutive days! Information regarding these races is available from USSA, 1750 E. Boulder Street, Colorado Springs, Colorado 80909.

On a worldwide scale, the Worldloppet is another series of nine races, ranging from 42 to 90 km in length. Included in this list are the Norwegian Birkebeiner, the U.S. Birkebeiner, Sweden's Vasaloppet, and the Riviera Rouge in Canada. You can get further information by writing Worldloppet, Cable, Wisconsin 54821.

Both race series are gaining in numbers of participants. The present leader seems to be Sweden's Vasa. The organizers have decided to cut the field at 12,000 for this one. Nevertheless, they frequently get 20,000 entries. There's a secretarial task for you . . . sending out those rejection slips! (Lots of colleges wouldn't mind this predicament.)

Many medal winners from the Olympic Games and the World Championships are racing in these big events. These skiers seem to get stronger and more adapted to long distances with age. Factories and companies have teams for these races and I expect this trend will continue in the future.

I've entered a couple of these events, in years past, before they became officially recognized as part of an international series. I can tell you that competing in these races is about the most fun thing going. But they are not anything to rush into without good preparation, both physical and mental.

Right now, the most important training I can do to prepare for a marathon is to make sure I don't set my sights too high and instead, make a vow to take it easy, pace myself, have fun, and know that I will enjoy finishing. If I approach any x-c event in this frame of mind I always enjoy it and I think my results are probably better than they would have been had I tried to "hurry" along.

Naturally, the physical training is important and not to be overlooked, but at this stage in my life I get more for my money with some of that "think training."

My advice to you would be to begin with short tour races in your area. See how you fare in these. As soon as you feel ready for the longer distances, make a commitment by entering a marathon, but do it months in advance. Then key for that event. Build slowly. Don't knock yourself out in your training, or in shorter races. Remember, you want to improve your capacities, not tear them down.

It usually helps to get a friend interested so you can train together occasionally, compare notes, and keep prodding each other if your enthusiasm fails.

Don't spare items or expenses that might cause you grief during or after the race. For instance, sleeping out in the snow is fine for a camping experience, but not for the night before a marathon.

If you're like me, once you try one of these marathons and finish successfully, you'll be hooked. What a high to take on a challenge like this and complete the tour! Usually, there is no end to the yarns when participants get together after the event to compare notes. If you look around at the right times, you'll find me there, too, somewhere.

## Where to Inquire

There are several good sources of information and I refer you to them. First, *The United States Ski Association* is the parent body for a host of committees which are concerned in some way with x-c. Most of the committees have divisional or regional members and you can get their names and addresses by writing the USSA, 1750 E. Boulder Street, Colorado Springs, Colorado 80909.

I list the committees, for your information: Cross-Country Committee, Nordic Advisory Committee, Nor Am Committee, Jumping Committee, Bill Koch Ski League Committee, Nordic Combined Committee, Junior Nordic Committee, Medical Committee, Points Committee, Course Approval Committee, Masters Committee, Ski Hill Engineering Committee, Cross-Country Officials Committee, Marathon Commission, Citizens Cross-Country Committee, Jumping Officials Committee.

To find out about qualifications necessary to enter a sanctioned race write either your USSA divisional office or your divisional Cross-Country Technical Committee. You can get both addresses from the USSA.

Recently, touring guides for several states and regions have been published. I've seen them for California, Michigan, Colorado, Minnesota, and New England, to name a few. Check your local bookstore for these.

Canada is similarly divided into divisions, each of which operates under Cross-Country Canada. For information on The Jackrabbit Program (skill development for children); Coaching, Officials, or Tour Leader Certification; or Loppets and Citizens' Races, write Cross-Country Canada, 333 River Road, Ottawa, Ontario K1L 8H9, Canada.

Canada has taken the lead in North America in having more complete x-c areas than the United States. A few complexes would qualify for the running of the Olympic Games with just a small amount of work. This in essence means there are a large number of wide, well-groomed trails. The tourskiers who go to Lake Placid benefit as a result of the recently held Olympic Games there.

# 10

# Going Out for All Day

AT HOME IN VERMONT we look forward to the springs when we can go out for some nice, easy, long tours on the corn snow. If the conditions are right the stone walls and most of the blowdowns are covered with snow, the woods are never more open, and you can stay on top of the snow. We usually take a leisurely start after breakfast and spend the day at it, returning home in the late afternoon. I'll hit on some of the procedures we use in this chapter. I realize that not all of you can do this sort of thing because of some kind of restriction. It could be impossible to do in your locality, or you might not have time, or you might not feel up to a venture like this. But if you really get into skiing it's within your realm.

For the extended backpacking tour, especially one that involves camping in high country like the Rockies, I recommend the Sierra Club totebook *Wilderness Skiing* by Steck and Tejada-Flores. It has lots of excellent information.

## How Far?

The distance can vary from a few kilometers to 40 or 50, depending on the skill of the group. Just a word of caution for everyone, however: Don't try to bite off more than you can chew. It's a good rule-of-thumb to plan any tour for a distance slightly shorter than you think can be easily managed by the least proficient skier of the group (or by anyone packing a small child). If you follow this tenet you'll be assured of completing the trip in good shape, with time to spare for unforeseen mishaps or hang-ups.

**98.** *Skiing in Oregon.*

## Who Can Go?

Never less than three, as for any other comparable trip over remote deep-country terrain.

More than ten, on the other hand, is rather a crowd, and ir eases the probability of having a few of the little problems that could slow down the parade.

It adds to the fun, though, to have a variety of ages. The stronger or more competent skiers can cruise back and forth, looking for the best route and tossing a good word to their slower-moving companions.

## The Leader

Someone has to be in charge. This person's judgment should be respected, for he is the one who might have to make a decision to turn back, or to deviate from the normal plan. Of course he should be an accomplished skier.

The leader must be familiar with the geography and the weather of the area. There's a lot of difference between a storm rolling in around the mountains of Vermont, say, and the Rockies. What holds for one area will not hold for another, and it follows that a transplanted expert skier will not necessarily make the best leader. Give consideration to the local talent. Many touring areas specialize in day trips like this and if you have any doubts about going it alone you should hire one of the professionals as a starter.

The leader must keep aware of the condition of the skiers in his group, and gear the speed to the slowest person. On long excursions a skier can run out of blood sugar and be unable to proceed for a period of time. In foul weather there is the danger of hypothermia. Any leader should be well versed in first aid and winter survival techniques and be ready to take action in any emergency situation.

## The Route

It's always a good idea for everyone to look at the planned route on a map. This is educational, it provides for a certain amount of incentive, and in case anyone does get lost it might make a big difference.

If you can plan the trip to follow the sun as much as possible it will make your trip more pleasant. For instance, if there's a choice between touring around the north side of a mountain, and the south, try the south. (Unless you're in the Southern Hemisphere. Or you want to avoid some wet snow on one side.)

If your route allows the possibility of beating a hasty retreat, all the better. Sometimes the weather socks in, or the group is not making the progress it expected to, and the wisest thing to do in this event is to head back to your beginning point.

## Trail Courtesy

A few years ago I didn't feel this section was necessary because then there were not many skiers and not many problems occurred. But now, it's probably a good idea to outline some generally accepted procedures for trail courtesy.

### TRAIL SIGNS

If you're skiing and you come across signs which tell you a trail is closed, or not to enter, or indicate that you are skiing the wrong direction, heed these warnings.

There are all sorts of reasons for closing trails, not the least of which is that the landowner might not want you on his property, but which

**99.** *Skiing in Oregon. Middle Sister is in the background.*

**100.** *A simple, clear method for marking trails at the Mt. St. Anne complex in Quebec.*

also include the management wanting to save the snow because of an upcoming event, or a poor weather forecast, or because a bridge is washed out farther down the trail.

Some skiers have problems understanding why a few trails are uni-directional. It's because they are unsafe going in the wrong direction. Around home we have lots of trails that I wouldn't be caught dead on—going the wrong way. Wrong way—no way—too hairy! (The ideal trail can be skiied in both directions, but terrain features often prevent this.)

If you ski down a short slope full of herringbone tracks, or if you find yourself doing a herringbone up a short, steep section where tracks indicate that everyone else has taken it straight, chances are good that you're going the wrong way. Turn around.

If you really study the marks made by others' pole baskets you can tell if you are skiing in the same direction as they were.

#### OTHER PERAMBULATORS

Any ski trail I know of has been designed for winter travel by skiers and for nothing else.

**101.** *Building which serves as timing "shack," race headquarters, warming "hut," and many more purposes at Mt. St. Anne, Quebec touring center.*

"Oh, can't I take my dog? He won't get in the way." No. A dog is a real menace on the trails. He can trip up other skiers and ruin the track without half trying. Some dogs get out in the backcountry on packed trails and then take off in pursuit of wildlife, like deer, and run them down and maul them.

Keep your dogs at home. You aren't doing anyone a favor, pets included, by taking them along.

### TRAIL MAINTENANCE

We all fall and it's a courtesy to other people using the trail to go back and fill in your sitzmark—even if you have paid the trail fee. If you have ever taken a fall because someone ahead of you did not fill his pothole, you can appreciate this situation.

### OTHER COURTESIES

If you are being overtaken on the trail, step to the side to allow the faster skier a chance to go ahead.

If you meet someone coming toward you on the trail, move to the right in order to pass.

If you're on your way up a hill and you meet someone coming down, give them the right of way.

138

I've argued this procedure with friends as it applies to cars on roads and I guess some states give the upcoming vehicle the right of way privilege. But with vehicles it's easy to see that those coming down have less control than those going up. And if one car is to back up, who has the easier job? On a snow-covered road there is no question here.

Skiers coming down a hill have less control than those coming up, so that's why I believe the skier coming down should have the right of way.

I have mentioned elsewhere the importance of getting permission to ski on someone's property. The worst thing you can do is to trespass on private property, damaging fences and leaving the mess from a fire built with the landowner's wood, plus garbage. If you do this in Vermont, be sure to stay out of shotgun range.

## Clothing

As I've said before, many light layers are better than one or two heavy ones. Be sure the clothes breathe. Gaiters are a must for touring in deep-snow country.

If you're going to be out for several hours don't skimp on little items

102. *Tracks like this are hard to beat for side-by-side skiing.*

like extra hats, headbands, gloves, and socks. These can easily fit in a small pack (or fannypack) and are well worth the trouble of bringing along.

If you need something bigger than a fannypack to carry your lunch and other supplies you can probably find a good pack in an outdoor equipment store. My favorite is the Norwegian Birkebeiner pack, designed especially for that race, where you carry a load of 5 kg. It has a small chest strap and is narrow enough to permit poling with ease.

One final bit of advice: Most experienced skiers try to pace themselves so as not to sweat heavily. If your clothes become soaked with perspiration you have to dry them before they will be of much use to you. The drying

**103.** *Local forester spends much of the day on skis in the early spring while he marks timber.*

can be difficult, especially if it turns much colder. So it's better to ski a little bit on the cool side, saving an extra wrap for colder weather or a long downhill run, rather than being too warm and sweating a lot. Wearing polypropelene underwear can help you avoid some of this problem of sweating and cooling.

## Eating

Your food can run the gamut from a sit-down affair at a cabin in the wilderness with grilled steak, wine, and the whole bit, to a few quick stops for a light snack. If the group is not in a hurry and can keep warm and comfortable during a lunch break, it sure is nice.

The trip should be planned so that water is available on the route; otherwise take liquids along. Liquid replacement during exercise is very important, and in the past too many skiers have neglected this in favor of eating, or taking in nothing at all. Mouthfuls of snow, allowed to melt before swallowing, will do in a pinch if you're not really thirsty.

Here are a few old standbys that we've had good luck with: Triscuits and peanuts; candy such as chocolate; cheese, raisins, apricots or other dried fruit; and oranges. This all fits in a fannypack or a frameless backpack and is easy to carry.

### CAMPFIRES

Quite a few years ago people never thought much of building a fire for lunch but nowadays the matters of conservation and pollution—not to mention consideration for the landowner, public or private—are important things to keep in mind. Therefore if you really want to have a fire you must plan ahead for it by inquiring in advance if a fire is permissible in a place you're thinking of. Many states, being heavily wooded, require that a fire permit be obtained from the local fire warden even though you've been given the O.K. by the institution or individual who owns the land. Statutes vary of course, so ask the fire marshal and local or state recreation and parks officials in your area what the requirements are.

And after a campfire picnic, or any pit-stop for that matter, anyone who likes unspoiled countryside enough to want to go skiing through it will leave behind only one thing: x-c tracks.

### APRÈS THE OUTING

When you get back home you'll be hungry again and if you've really planned things well it will be an easy matter to put out another spread without waiting, or having one or two people feel obliged to spend an hour in food preparation.

No one in our family ever wanted to stay home just to tend the stove, so we start a soup going before we leave. Soup bones, stew meat, stewed tomatoes, celery, carrots, onions, bouillon cubes, bay leaf—and anything else left in the icebox—make a good starter. There's always some homemade bread on hand and spreads like peanut butter, cheese, jam, etc. All these dishes are easily expanded and we can handle a crowd of a dozen with aplomb.

## Non-Food Equipment

In addition to food, someone in the group should take a few waxing and ski repair items like: A spare plastic or metal ski tip (good for digging in the night), a cake of paraffin and the next softest ski wax you might need, a combination knife/screwdriver, small roll of adhesive tape, matches, a candle, a scraper; and some wire.

If you're a camera bug, by all means take some pictures of your little trips. You'll get even more kick out of viewing the pictures as the years go by.

Taking overnight trips, complete with sleeping bags, tents, cooking utensils, etc., is another matter which I am not going to cover. I like camping, but in the winter I prefer to put most of my energy into skiing.

## Ideas for Other Trips

If you're part of a larger group which includes two cars, take a crossover trip. Park the cars at opposite ends of your route, have each group meet in the middle of the tour for lunch, and proceed.

Don't forget to exchange car keys at lunch.

### ORIENTEERING

Get hold of some pamphlets or the book *Orienteering for Sport and Pleasure* by Bengtsson and Atkinson, and set up a course for that.

This is a very popular sport in Scandinavia which combines map-reading and skiing skills. It's a good way to learn to read maps, and you'll need compasses for this.

You can get maps of new territory and explore it, without compasses. This is fun and it's O.K. so long as it isn't snowing so as to wipe out your ski tracks. I'd hate to get lost and not have tracks to follow back to my starting point.

### NIGHT SKIING

Night skiing on lighted tracks is gaining here in North America and, if you get a chance, you should try it. Better yet, try to get a group together to build your own little loop. String up some carnival lights, use street lights, automobile headlights, bonfires, torches, or anything that will provide some illumination.

Once or twice a year, when there is a little powder snow on top of a good base, and the moon is full, we go out night skiing. This is some thrill!

You know those bright nights when you can see your shadow on the snow? Try it. It's quite good for your balance, since you can't see all the very small ripples in the track and you have to learn to relax and absorb the little bumps.

Finally, if you don't have a lighted track, and the moon isn't just right for you, get a headlamp of the sort miners traditionally have used and go out on your own. These are on the market now and are very handy. The lamp is light, attaches to your head with a headband, and is powered by a battery pack which you carry on your belt.

Here's one situation where you'll want to avoid a lot of bobbing of the head, or bouncing around looking from side to side. If you want to see where you're going you'll have to keep the lamp pointed directly, and steadily, ahead.

## Group Activities

Many skiers go out in groups and if you want to have some fun while staying together and keeping warm, or active, you can try some of these activities.

Usually, there is one person who acts as leader or "coach" and while this is not a necessity, it will help to organize matters if someone assumes this role.

I've never felt hampered by playing kids' games like follow-the-leader. It can take you through hardwood groves, over bumpy terrain, under fences or low-hanging branches. When we get going late in the season we try to make a contest of it by seeing how quickly we can brush off the followers by ducking under low-hanging branches, or making quick, sharp, last-minute turns, or jumping stone walls. This can be a real gas for adults, since they seem to get more laughs out of it than the kids do.

Pairing skiers of near-equal ability is a good method to keep everyone moving, especially on a cold day. Have the skiers compare various elements of their technique, like the length of stride, the strength (length) of their double-poling efforts, etc.

A really good method for comparing the virtues of different skis' bottoms and wax jobs is to climb a hill and take a straight run down to see who coasts the farthest. You can build some friendly competition this way and get a fair amount of practice climbing hills, as well.

Then you can turn around and determine who has the best climbing skis, or technique, by seeing who can ski the farthest straight up the hill . . . without poles, of course.

Then see who can climb straight up the farthest, using his arms. This

**104.** *Some locals strike out for a tour in fresh snow during sugar season.*

may tell you who has the strongest arms, but not necessarily the best climb.

Pick out a corner which requires a step turn, a skate turn, or even a stem turn, and practice it. You might find it advantageous to ride around the outside of the corner taking short step-turns, where someone else might prefer a couple of good skates and an inside line.

Setting up a slalom on a very flat incline is a good way to bring out the various downhill abilities in the group.

I have skiers go abreast, through unbroken snow, and then study their tracks for quirks. Some tracks will wander a fair amount, with the distance between the skis varying, while others will look straight and true.

## Precautions

After writing so much about cross-country, joys of, it's time to make note of a few things that can go wrong. I like to "think positive" and all that, but I feel obligated to mention the dangers that some people have encountered. And with millions of people taking up x-c, it's no wonder that a few have some scrapes now and then. Let me first discuss

144

two health problems which may affect x-c skiers, namely *hypothermia* and *frostbite*.

## HYPOTHERMIA

Hypothermia is a condition in which the body is unable to maintain its core temperature of about 99° F. If the cooling of the body is severe, death can result. So if you are out with a group and someone gets hypothermic you are in a real pickle. Before I talk about the symptoms and treatment it's a good idea to review the conditions that can cool your body or lead to hypothermia. Obviously, the point is to avoid these conditions.

The body loses heat by conduction and an example of this is caused by wearing wet, cold clothing next to your skin, or worse, being immersed in cold water. If your clothing gets wet, change into dry garments.

When air moves across body surfaces we lose heat by convection. A stiff wind can cause a large loss of heat, so wear windbreakers. (See Windchill Chart on the next page.)

As water evaporates from the body's surface it absorbs heat from the body and this is another way we lose heat. It follows that if there is a danger from hypothermia you should not move so fast that you cause sweating. In addition, lots of exercise will burn up your food or fuel supplies and without reserves you are in a more precarious situation. One of the rules for cold weather existence is to eat plenty of food. Your body needs it. Don't worry about gaining a few ounces of weight here and there.

Your body also loses heat by radiation and this amount is related to the body's surface area.

Generalizing, hypothermia usually is accompanied by some of the following conditions: exhaustion, lack of food, injury (being forced to lie in the snow and/or suffering from shock), inadequate or wet clothing.

In sum, to best protect yourself from hypothermia, take in plenty of food—especially carbohydrates, which are most easily burned as fuel by the body—protect yourself from the wind, insulate yourself from the cold, don't allow yourself to get too tired, and get rid of any perspiration by wearing clothing which will wick it, or by changing clothes as often as necessary.

## SYMPTOMS

The early symptoms of hypothermia are like those of fatigue. However, in many cases the victim's judgment soon becomes impaired and he seems unconcerned and unaware of his condition. It's most important that a victim's companions are able to recognize these symptoms.

Other symptoms include a numbness of the skin, shivering, and a loss of muscle coordination.

# WINDCHILL CHART

| WIND SPEED | | COOLING POWER OF WIND ON EXPOSED FLESH EXPRESSED AS AN EQUIVALENT TEMPERATURE | | | | | | | | |
|---|---|---|---|---|---|---|---|---|---|---|
| KNOTS | MPH | ACTUAL THERMOMETER READING | | | | | | | | |
| CALM | CALM | F | 40 | 35 | 30 | 25 | 20 | 15 | 10 | 5 | 0 |
| | | C | 4 | 2 | −1 | −4 | −7 | −9 | −12 | −15 | −18 |
| | | EQUIVALENT TEMPERATURE | | | | | | | | |
| 3–6 | 5 | F | 35 | 30 | 25 | 20 | 15 | 10 | 5 | 0 | −5 |
| | | C | 2 | −1 | −4 | −7 | −9 | −12 | −15 | −18 | −21 |
| 7–10 | 10 | F | 30 | 20 | 15 | 10 | 5 | 0 | −10 | −15 | −20 |
| | | C | −1 | −7 | −9 | −12 | −15 | −18 | −23 | −26 | −29 |
| 11–15 | 15 | F | 25 | 15 | 10 | 0 | −5 | −10 | −20 | −25 | −30 |
| | | C | −4 | −9 | −12 | −18 | −21 | −23 | −29 | −32 | −34 |
| 16–19 | 20 | F | 20 | 10 | 5 | 0 | −10 | −15 | −25 | −30 | −35 |
| | | C | −7 | −12 | −15 | −18 | −23 | −26 | −32 | −34 | −37 |
| 20–23 | 25 | F | 15 | 10 | 0 | −5 | −15 | −20 | −30 | −35 | −45 |
| | | C | −9 | −12 | −18 | −21 | −26 | −29 | −34 | −37 | −43 |
| 24–28 | 30 | F | 10 | 5 | 0 | −10 | −20 | −25 | −30 | −40 | −50 |
| | | C | −12 | −15 | −18 | −23 | −29 | −32 | −34 | −40 | −46 |
| 29–32 | 35 | F | 10 | 5 | −5 | −10 | −20 | −30 | −35 | −40 | −50 |
| | | C | −12 | −15 | −21 | −23 | −29 | −34 | −37 | −40 | −46 |
| 33–36 | 40 | F | 10 | −0 | −5 | −15 | −20 | −30 | −35 | −45 | −55 |
| | | C | −12 | −18 | −21 | −26 | −29 | −34 | −37 | −43 | −48 |

| WINDS ABOVE 40 MPH HAVE LITTLE ADDITIONAL EFFECT | LITTLE DANGER (for properly clothed person) Maximum danger is false sense of security. | INCREASING DANGER Danger from freezing of exposed flesh. (flesh may freeze within one minute) |
|---|---|---|
| | Trenchfoot and Immersion Foot May Occur at Any Point on This Cha | |

From: *Arctic Medical Research Lab, Fairbanks, Alaska.*
*Prepared by Department of the Navy.*

ACTUAL THERMOMETER READING

| −5 | −10 | −15 | −20 | −25 | −30 | −35 | −40 | −45 | −50 | −55 | −60 |
|---|---|---|---|---|---|---|---|---|---|---|---|
| −21 | −23 | −26 | −29 | −32 | −34 | −37 | −40 | −43 | −46 | −48 | −51 |

EQUIVALENT TEMPERATURE

| −10 | −15 | −20 | −25 | −30 | −35 | −40 | −45 | −50 | −55 | −60 | −70 |
|---|---|---|---|---|---|---|---|---|---|---|---|
| −23 | −26 | −29 | −32 | −34 | −37 | −40 | −43 | −46 | −48 | −51 | −57 |
| −25 | −35 | −40 | −45 | −50 | −60 | −65 | −70 | −80 | −85 | −90 | −95 |
| −32 | −37 | −40 | −43 | −46 | −51 | −54 | −57 | −62 | −65 | −68 | −71 |
| −40 | −45 | −50 | −60 | −65 | −70 | −80 | −85 | −90 | −100 | −105 | −110 |
| −40 | −43 | −46 | −51 | −54 | −57 | −62 | −65 | −68 | −73 | −76 | −79 |
| −45 | −50 | −60 | −65 | −75 | −80 | −85 | −95 | −100 | −110 | −115 | −120 |
| −43 | −46 | −51 | −54 | −60 | −62 | −65 | −71 | −73 | −79 | −81 | −84 |
| −50 | −60 | −65 | −75 | −80 | −90 | −95 | −105 | −100 | −120 | −125 | −135 |
| −46 | −51 | −54 | −60 | −62 | −68 | −71 | −76 | −79 | −84 | −87 | −93 |
| −55 | −65 | −70 | −80 | −85 | −95 | −100 | −110 | −115 | −125 | −130 | −140 |
| −48 | −54 | −57 | −62 | −65 | −71 | −73 | −79 | −81 | −87 | −90 | −96 |
| −60 | −65 | −75 | −80 | −90 | −100 | −105 | −115 | −120 | −130 | −135 | −145 |
| −51 | −54 | −60 | −62 | −68 | −73 | −76 | −81 | −84 | −90 | −93 | −98 |
| −60 | −70 | −75 | −85 | −95 | −100 | −110 | −115 | −125 | −130 | −140 | −150 |
| −51 | −57 | −60 | −65 | −71 | −73 | −79 | −81 | −87 | −90 | −96 | −101 |

GREAT DANGER
(flesh may freeze within
30 seconds)

TREATMENT

The methods of treatment obviously depend on your situation, but even then there is some controversy.

If you can get the victim to a hospital in short order this is probably the best. If the victim is unconscious you *must* get him to a hospital as soon as possible.

The patient's core temperature must be raised and in severe cases his body is unable to do this. So, he needs help.

Keep the patient quiet. Warm liquids are suggested. Skin to skin contact, especially in the trunk area, is also indicated. Put a warm person in a sleeping bag with the victim, or wrap both people in blankets. Alcohol and smoking will both have negative effects on the warming process.

## Frostbite

Most people who live in cold climates are familiar with frostbite. Around here some of the skiers are particularly susceptible to it since they have suffered from frostbite before.

The skin usually turns white at the frostbitten area and immediate warming is indicated. If you're outside, far from a warm place, it's good to thaw the area with someone's warm hands.

We often associate frostbite with windchill, windchill being the combination of cold and air moving by. I say "air moving by" because on a cold, calm day it's easy to get a serious windchill factor by skiing fast down a long hill. So don't think you are safe from windchill just because the wind is not blowing. You can plug in your skiing speeds to the chart on pages 146–147.

More serious frostbite, or deep frostbite, should be treated at a hospital. It's generally believed that if someone freezes his hands or feet it's best to move them to a hospital just that way. In other words, don't thaw the parts, then take a chance on them freezing up again before reaching help. This worsens the problem. Skiers have skied out with frozen feet and apparently have not complicated the condition by doing so.

Large numbers of skiers spend most of their time at touring areas . . . areas complete with marked trails, maps, groomed tracks, trail sweeps, and other safety features. There are very few accidents in these situations. There shouldn't be. That's the way it's planned.

On the other hand, cross-country skiing is an umbrella term sometimes used in connection with wilderness skiing, mountaineering, downhill cross-country, Telemarking, one-day tours, exploring, and overnight camping. These are situations where you are more likely to encounter problems.

The fact is, anytime you venture forth in the winter, you are taking a certain risk and should be well prepared for it. Being prepared means knowing about the risks and knowing what to do to avoid them, or what to do if something untoward happens.

## Getting Lost

Getting lost is often merely a preliminary to something else more serious. How often have you heard someone exclaim that the group was doing well until it got lost. Actually, the group was not doing well from the very beginning. It shouldn't have got lost. Someone did not plan well.

Many novices think that a map and compass is the answer to keep from getting lost. Map and compass work is the name of the game in orienteering, but that is quite a different situation from that of taking a long tour through unknown territory. The knowledgeable hikers will tell you that landmarks are so important and the clear implication is that you should know the landmarks you are looking for. To go further, if you embark on a trip where no one in the group is familiar with the terrain, you are just asking for trouble.

*It goes without saying*—I hope—*that you should not go on long tours alone.* You could get lost, or merely sprain an ankle, and be stuck out there, alone. Think about that one.

## Being Lost

O.K., you blew it and you're lost. What do you do?

There are no hard and fast rules for this situation. However, proper planning for any trip by necessity includes studying and knowing how to spend the night out. A good drill would be to practice this right near your home, a lodge, or a shelter.

Unfortunately, many lessons we learn are the result of disasters. "If only they had dug in for the night." Or, "If only they had pushed on just another mile they would have found shelter."

Most people, who have never spent a night out in the winter and who know nothing about it, are ill-prepared to do it, especially if they are lost at the end of a day's tour.

I've never been in an emergency situation like this, but I have done some winter camping, and so I think I could make it. Here's what I would do.

First, I would determine how much energy we could spend trying to get some shelter. Being lost, this would be difficult in most situations. It wouldn't take much to decide that chances of survival were better by conserving energy and digging in for the night, rather than pushing on to exhaustion and then trying to dig in.

A snow cave is a wonderful shelter, but without trying to sound flip, most of the people who know how to dig snow caves don't get lost in the bush during winter. So I would toss out that possibility for most people. But a snow trench is another thing. It's easier to dig and takes less energy.

Find a sheltered place where there is good snow depth and start digging. You may have to use the tip of your ski if you don't have anything else, like a fold-up shovel, or a spare ski tip. Make the trench deep enough so you can put in boughs, or something on the bottom to sit on and insulate you from the snow, and still have headroom under the roof. For the roof, cover the opening with your poles, skis, more boughs, and then finish it with snow. The snow will act as insulation.

Climb into the trench, try to rig something across the end to keep the air from blowing through—but leave ventilation holes—huddle together, and you will make it through the night.

Next day you can hope for better bearings, or that someone will miss you and come searching. If the weather and visibility are really bad you should consider spending another night out. You can survive another day quite easily without food, but be sure to get some water, even if it means melting snow in your mouth.

One of the keys in a winter emergency is to conserve energy. Wear all your clothing, restrict your movements, use anything available for a windbreak, drink running, cold water rather than melting snow in your mouth, etc.

If you are ever stuck like this you are bound to begin asking yourself questions, such as the following:

Did we tell someone where we were going and when we expected to return?

If so, were our directions good enough so they can find us?

Can we backtrack tomorrow and at least get to our starting point?

What was it that we are supposed to do to increase chances of survival?

To repeat, a few hours' study and some practical experience is one of the best investments you can make if you run even the slightest risk of getting into a situation like this.


## Avalanches

While the most serious avalanche dangers occur in the higher mountains of western North America it would be a mistake to consider yourself immune from one in the eastern sections. Several years ago, for instance, at the beginning of the annual Harvard-Dartmouth Slalom Race at Hillman's Highway on Mt. Washington, two skiers triggered an avalanche high above the course and a five-to-eight-foot wall of snow thundered down the slope. Fortunately, almost all the skiers were off to the side waiting for the first competitor, and no one got caught in the slide.

It goes without saying that if you are going to ski in avalanche country you should learn as much as you can about avalanche conditions, what causes avalanches, and how you can avoid them. In addition, you should take the necessary precautions in the event you are caught in one.

I'll just make a few remarks, but these aren't meant to take the burden off you to learn more about avalanches.

Most avalanches occur on steep slopes of 30 degrees or more. They typically occur after powder snowstorms and can be caused by skiers traversing, or cutting across, the slope. U- and V-shaped gullies are prone to slide.

Try to avoid routes that take you across these areas. If you must cross them, send one person at a time and if a slide does occur, watch him carefully.

You should have avalanche cords and beepers if you ski regularly in avalanche country.

If you are skiing across a slope which has avalanche potential you should always have an escape route in mind. The best possibility would usually be to ski down and across the slope as fast as you can. Not many people outski avalanches, however good reading material it might make.

If you get caught in an avalanche you should try to stay oriented and upright. As the slide slows protect your face with your hands in order to create some breathing space by digging when it stops. Stretch one arm straight upward in the hope it will provide a marker for searchers in the event you are buried. If you panic and thrash around, burning up the available oxygen faster than necessary, you may lessen your chances for survival.

I've never been caught in an avalanche and I don't intend to practice this event just so I can write about swimming to the top of the snow, or wishing perhaps that my skis and poles had not been so firmly attached to my limbs. My best advice to you is not to get caught.

See appendix for additional good reading on avalanches.

### WHITE-OUTS

Unless you've been in a white-out it's difficult to believe the descriptions you hear of them.

White-outs occur when snow is falling, blowing around, or both. Visibility is near zero and it's almost impossible to distinguish ups from downs as you move along. I've been in a couple of these while skiing and once led the 1952 Olympic Team over a 20-foot drop in the Sun Valley golf course during a training session. For an instant I thought I had fallen into space, forever.

If you get caught in a white-out the preferred procedure is to wait it out. If this is impractical, proceed very slowly and try to find some shelter where you can wait it out. If you are skiing in a group and can rope together it will help prevent someone from getting separated. If you can't rope together, then use frequent voice signals to keep in touch.

## Things to be Careful About

Don't get spoiled by good racing trails, or area x-c trails which are well laid out and well groomed. If you're out in the boonies, be prepared. Zinging down a hill with a carefree attitude is fine, but it can lead to difficulties. The end of a long downhill section may take you into a washout, or a fallen-in bridge, or a sharp corner that's not negotiable, or a blowdown.

### BRIDGES AND BROOKS

There are all sorts of methods for crossing bridges that are in need of repair and otherwise. I can, from experience, list a few things *not* to do.

1. Don't try to use your poles on a slatted bridge, lest a point stick in between the slats and you break the pole or wrench your arm.
2. Don't try to ski directly across a bridge where your skis will get caught between loose planks or small logs. You're likely to end up with one foot sticking through, possibly down in the water. Don't ever be afraid to take off your skis and walk across or around the bridge, or the brook.
3. If there is a thin film of water at a crossing, ski through it *without* lifting your ski from the snow. If you lift the ski and then put it down again in the snow on the other side of the crossing, your skis will probably ice up—and they could stay that way for the rest of the trip.

### ROAD CROSSINGS

Around our area most of the skiers have perfected the one-legged-road-crossing technique. They boom up to a road, take off one ski, and hop across the road on that free foot, carrying the other ski in their hand.

Why not take off both skis and walk across the road, as a normal person would? Good question. I guess it's quicker to do it by hopping on one foot; and anyway it's a bit of a challenge.

### FENCES

Beautiful. The first skier zips across a barbed-wire fence, and disappears into the yonder. Following skiers will attack the fence in an effort to keep up. They'll get hung up on top of the strands, underneath the strands; one person will lift one strand while another farther down the line steps on it; and so on.

Saner people take their time, survey the situation, perhaps take off their skis, and get through or over the fence in the easiest manner.

## Wrap Up

No activity, including cross-country skiing, is safe from accidents. Some activities have lower risks than others and doctors and statisticians bask in figures purporting to favor one sport over another. I don't go for these reports and don't worry too much about their findings. But I do try to prevent accidents and *maybe* I worry too much.

In my mind there has always been a fine line dividing the foolhardy activities from the boringly-safe ones. It's easy to play quarterback-after-the-event and state that an accident could have been avoided. But how difficult it is to state how much faster, farther, higher, one could have gone after an accident-free outing.

I'm lucky. My joints and various parts have been repaired during five operations and I'm still fairly functional. I have great faith in the medical profession and am willing to take on the risks involved with the sports I engage in. What the heck—presidents break collarbones skiing, x-c authors get their legs punctured by ski tips, people break legs, and so on, but this doesn't do much to detract from the wonderful sport of cross-country.

# 11

# Citraces and Local Races

THE GROWTH OF CITIZEN'S races, marathons, loppets, or whatever they are called has naturally been accompanied by a big growth in qualified race organizers and officials. Some of the races have become extravaganzas, complete with entertainments and services we never dreamed of for the entrants.

In general, the demands of putting on a citizen's race, or more simply, a ski association race, have increased so much that many smaller organizations are unable to run these contests. They lack the proper facilities such as wide trails, parking places, and ample toilets, or they don't have the track-setting equipment necessary to condition the course properly. At the same time, some of the more established citizen's races are dropping off in popularity and now get fields of only a few hundred. The reasons for this are unclear at this writing, but it could be that the average citracer has had enough competition, or that the entry fees have been a deterrent (sometimes these are in excess of $50). Around here we sometimes calculate the cost per kilometer for the races we enter and it usually turns out that the Eastern Ski Association races offer the best bargain. The tracks are usually adequate, the trails good enough (sometimes narrow enough to bring on a few thrills), and the organizers give out the times and refreshments. For many racers these are the basic requirements.

I want to put in a plug for bringing back the local races, or tours . . . the ones organized by a club, a town or a community. The amount of hoopla you get involved in is entirely your choice but let's see how easy it is to cover the essentials.

**105–107.** *Three pictures showing some of the evolution of tour-racing in the United States. Top: early Washington's Birthday Race in Guilford, Vermont. Middle: start of the Waterville Valley Marathon. Bottom: Start of the 1984 Birkebeiner in Telemark, Wisconsin.*

## Tour or Race?

You could decide on a tour and set up a time to begin and leave it at that. In this case you should refer to some of the points mentioned in Chapter 10, Going Out for All Day.

Or you could offer the tour during a block of time in the middle of the day and let the skiers go when they want to.

If you want to call it a race, complete with times, you will have to be more definite about start times. Interval starts are the most common with small fields but you shouldn't be bound by this notion. You could start the racers in waves or groups, according to age, sex, or any other classification.

In every case, be sure to have a postrunner or two to sweep the course after the day's activities.

### FOR THE COURSE

Some races use a loop, or trail, that begins and ends in the same place. This is like most cross-country ski races.

Some races are run from one location to another. I prefer this kind, even if only for the psychological reason of going somewhere. It's nice to be able to say, for instance, that I toured across a town line or two.

Many citizens' races use the same trail every year. This way, skiers can compare times from one year to another, and even though snow conditions are faster some years than others, it makes for an interesting addition to the race.

The length of the courses varies from a few kilometers to the real long ones—like Sweden's Vasa, which is 85 km. A standard that is popular on this continent is between 10 and 15 km. However, if you have a nifty course in mind which might go longer you shouldn't worry about it too much. Advertise the length, and any tourskier who thinks it's a bit too long should take it easy, or not enter the race. Even a course of 30–40 km shouldn't give the practiced tourskier much trouble if he paces himself.

### FOR THE FIELD

Most of the races have been open to anyone who can ski x-c over the course. If you have some real beginners you could send them off with a few more expert skiers, especially if you are using a tour format, and the jaunt could include instruction along the way.

### ENTRY FEES

If the tour or the race is very local in nature you have several options open. Any expenses incurred ought to be covered and if you agree beforehand to take the money out of the club treasury (If your treasury can afford it!) then there's no need for an entry.

**108.** *When you're desperate for a race you truck snow in and spread it around an athletic field.*

Or, if you have some energetic people on your organizing committee, send them out looking for a sponsor. You can offer pre-race publicity, bibs bearing the sponsor's name alongside the title of the race, results printed on the sponsor's stationery, and so on. Even a small financial cushion in the form of guarantees toward expenses can make the going much easier.

Name to this chore only those who really know the community or the outside persons being solicited, and assign the specific people to be called on. Or, you could ask for donations.

Or, you could have a sliding scale of fees which make it less expensive for the younger skiers, or for the families, etc.

Or, you could ask each entrant to donate something for the prize table, or for the potluck meal which follows the event. The idea is to keep it low-key and local.

### THE TRAIL COMMITTEE

The trail location should be determined during the off-season, well before snowtime. It should be cut and cleared—and measured, because everyone wants to know how far he skied. It is particularly important to avoid steep downhills, and all downhill sections should be followed by a straight, flat outrun. And you'll have fewer maintenance problems if the trail is out of the wind and if there aren't too many sections facing the south sun.

Ideally, the loop type of trail should be ⅓ uphill, ⅓ level and ⅓ downhill. If you are going from one location to another, though, you'll probably attract more skiers if you use a downhill route—i.e., if there's an altitude difference between the start and finish points, choose the lower ground for the finish.

### FIRST: MANNERS

After you've got the course in mind, you do what is the most important thing of all: *Call in person on landowners and get their permission for the race to cross their property.* You should have insurance, and therefore be able to assure each landowner that he is not liable for damages in case of a mishap. If he wants his land used *only* for the period of the race, this fact must be made clear later on to all entrants (some of whom might otherwise want to train on the course beforehand). Of course any cutting, leveling, or clearing to make a good trail must also be O.K.'d in advance.

In return, remember that it never hurts to repair fences or cut up some fireplace wood for people whose land you use. Finally, after the race is over, don't forget formal thanks.

### WITH TOOLS IN HAND

Some shoveling or bulldozing may be necessary to smooth the trail. Sidehill sections where one ski is lower than the other are to be avoided, both from a skier's and a track-setter's standpoint.

On certain stretches you should think of how snow will weigh down tree branches hanging over the heads of skiers who are on a trail a couple of feet deep in snow. Then you'll realize that clearing limbs and brush to a height of 2 meters isn't enough. Get the tall persons in the trail-clearing group to do the high work.

### RACE SECRETARY

I always use this person as the catch-all. You'll see why when you read further. There are lots of odd jobs that can be done and, while some of them might logically be done by someone else, I've chosen to put them here for emphasis.

There are the ordinary duties of getting entries, arranging for whatever prizes are decided on, making up the running order or assigning bib numbers, handing out numbers on the race day (and collecting them if this is necessary), keeping times and scoring results, and typing them up.

PRIZES AND AWARDS

In our club we've never made a big deal out of prizes, sensing that the tourskier's reward comes from doing the race rather than collecting a doodad to display in his corner cupboard. Even the local hotshots on the U.S. Team who have run in our tours feel the same way, enjoying the carefree competition.

We did obtain a permanent trophy and engraved the name of the overall winner on it for several years, as much to keep a record as for anything else.

Always, though, the emphasis was on an inexpensive small memento to be given each finisher. In addition, there have been modest prizes—chosen to be useful—for class winners. These have been such things as wax, wax remover, corks, gadgets like that.

GROUP SCORING

In some of the tour races in Scandinavia they use a scoring system for clubs. This can be as simple as, say, taking the first few finishing places from each club, with the low-total group winning a rotating trophy; or, the high-score club may provide the refreshments at the next get-together; or, bonus points can be awarded for family participation or for the younger or older members.

ARRANGING FOR WAX INFORMATION

If you can find a coach or some veteran racers who are willing to stick their necks out and prescribe wax for the competitors, it makes for a nice gesture. Lots of tourskiers admit to being in the dark about waxing and are grateful for any advice they can get.

If there are elevation changes in your course, and you want to be really flossy, you can post air temperatures, as recorded along the course, for help with waxing previous to the race. This would be most helpful for those who are waxing on their own, possibly disregarding any official waxing information given by someone in the know.

## Track Preparation

The best way to prepare tracks for x-c skiing is by using a snowmobile, or some snow-compacting machine, and a track sled.

Ideally, the swath you pack should be 3 to 4 meters wide. If you use a wave start you should have some parallel tracks for the first 1–2 km on the course. If you have a really big field you'll have to make the trail wider and set more tracks. At Vasloppet in Sweden they set several parallel tracks for all 85 km.

The tracks themselves should be set so there is about 12 centimeters between the inside edges of each ski. If you want to get real fancy you can follow the FIS standards, which call for a distance between inside edges of 12–18 cm on the flat and 8–12 cm on the uphills. (When you ski uphill it is normal to run with skis closer together).

Don't bother to put tracks in around corners or on downhill turns. It is better to pack the snow well in these sections and let the skiers make their own skate-turn marks, etc.

### USING THE TRAIL EQUIPMENT

There are several hints I can give which should be helpful. In our area we have had lots of experience with snow-packing and have learned many things the hard way. The comments I make will be appropriate for machines like our snowmobile—an Alpine—and our track sled. If you have a Snocat, then you're in a different league: You can use a much bigger sled and do a better job.

First of all, be careful. Running a snowmobile can be exhausting work.

**109.** *An all-in-one track-maker: the rigid drum packs the trail, the sled sets the tracks.*

Getting stuck out there in the boondocks and having to lift the machine out of deep snow, holes, or from in between trees is rugged. Be sure to take along a shovel and an axe whenever you go far from any roads.

*Level trails.* If your trail is level, it will make for easier snowmobiling. The machines aren't too effective crossways on sidehills, even when you lean out and make like an outrigger to keep them going straight up or down. In fact, if you have a lot of sidehill terrain you are in for a few thrills. During the summer we chip away at our sidehills with shovels or bulldozers, gouging skiable shelves across the faces of the hills.

*Watch out for dips in the trail.* It's those small ones that get you: the runners on the machine are headed uphill, the tail end is headed downhill, and the drive belt is suspended, spinning madly. Fill the dips in. They might be ski-breakers anyway.

*Pack the trail after every snowfall of six inches or so.* If you wait until you have a depth of two feet of unpacked snow it will be very difficult to pack the trail, particularly the uphill sections. Most of the snowmobiles don't lack power, as you may know, but they do need traction.

*Working on uphills.* There are a couple of methods we use for our uphills. If the snow is deep even after one storm, we take two vehicles out and play leapfrog. One goes uphill as far as it can without getting stuck, peels off and returns to the foot. The other vehicle follows the first's tracks and can get up farther before peeling off and coming back.

Another system is to run the course so that you can take the steep uphills going downhill, by traveling in the reverse direction.

In deep snow situations, if you can't run the course backwards as above, or take the hills the way you would like to, it often helps to footpack up the hill before trying it with the machine. One trip up and back will usually do the trick.

You should never pack a trail during warm weather if you know freezing weather will follow soon.

WHEN TO PUT IN THE TRACK

When you pack a trail be sure not to let it set up, or freeze, too long before putting in the track. The best system is to drag the track sled right behind the machine, and pack and set the track at the same time. This may not be possible because of the snow depth or the terrain. If it isn't, do a small section of packing, then set the track. If you wait until the next day, the packed snow may be too hard. This is especially likely to happen if there is a lot of moisture in the snow, as in the East.

If you have to go around a few times before setting the track, leave for the last trip the middle section where you intend to set track. Then attach the sled and set the track.

If your machine is powerful enough and the conditions are right, you can drag a skier on a towrope behind the track sled. This gives you the perfect system. It is important to ski in the tracks set by the sled soon

**110.** *The Olympic races at Sarajevo, Yugoslavia, had beautiful surroundings to ski in.*

after they're made. The tracks freeze and, if they are not skied in, some ski bindings will catch on the sides when the first skiers use the tracks later on.

If the track is set and things warm up, keep the skiers off. (It's a good idea to post the trail before the race anyway.)

If this is not possible, then here's a neat trick that will save your track. Just as the weather starts to cool, or after the skiers are done with the track, go around it with the snowmobile and a big, heavy chain looped behind the snowmobile. The chain will wipe out the old track, or fill it in, and leave your trail looking like a new carpet. After the weather freezes you will have a loose granular condition instead of two icy ruts. Then weight the track sled if necessary and go around it again.

162

## SETTING TRACKS IN ICE

In very icy conditions race organizers would be wise to run a short loop with a well-prepared track, rather than attempt to condition a long stretch of trail. (My Western friends grin when they read about icy tracks. But when you live in the East one of the first things you learn is to deal with situations like this.)

There are many different sleds for use in icy conditions, and most of them operate on the harrow principle. They are heavy and have a bunch of sharp, cutting edges that stick down into the crust and cut it up.

We've even used bulldozers to crush the crust.

But it's worth another warning. Some of the best-known races have turned into nightmares for many competitors because of icy conditions and you should be very careful about holding competitions in these conditions. If there is any doubt, postpone it. Or cancel. The problem is, most competitors are trusting or naive and believe that if a race is being held, things must be O.K.

## The Timers

You need someone with a cool head here to take over the timing crew. We've had good luck with math teachers in our neck of the woods, or local businessmen who know their numbers.

## Various Timing Methods

*The honor system.* The racer shows at the start, logs in his starting time and, on completion of the course, logs in his finish time. If the course has different start and finish points, the timers must synchronize some watches; or start the race and hightail it to the finish before any racers show up. Or you could start the race by radio or telephone if this is convenient.

*An electric timer.* Complete with electric eye and a punch-out tape which records the times, this makes the most accurate method of timing. These timers are certainly not necessary for casual tour races, but they are required for important meets like the National Championships, where many officials feel that the utmost in accuracy is necessary.

I don't want to get too much into the theory of this, but there is no accuracy advantage in using an electric timer unless you can start the race with it.

*Opting for chronometer plus stopwatches.* The most common method of timing these races is by using a mass start and a couple of stopwatches and a chronometer, or master clock. Ideally, you start all the racers simultaneously, using your chronometer and at least one other watch as a back-up. Then when the racers finish, record their times with the chronometer. If you want split-second accuracy, start a stopwatch on the minute, using the chronometer, when you see a racer coming into sight; stop the watch when the racer finishes, and read his time. It might be something like 27.4 seconds on your watch, and you add this to the chronometer time at which you started your stopwatch.

## The Computer Age

Naturally, at big races like the Olympics and the World Championships, the timing and publication of results is very sophisticated. They have electric timing tied right in with a computer which can signal a scoreboard and instruct it to post interval times, or finish times in order at any point in the race, or print-outs can be obtained during and after the race. It's efficient and accurate and takes much of the human element right out of the whole process. It's come to be expected at these meets.

Let's not pooh-pooh some of this approach for use during club races. There are lots of computer jocks around and many of them would gladly accept the challenge of writing a program to give you print-outs of your results. Many schools in our area have had such programs for a couple of years and they sure are impressive.

## The Recorders

The recorders are the ones who note the second a racer crosses the finish line and write it on a slip of paper, along with the racer's bib number and the minute he crossed the line.

Meanwhile, one timer has the sole job of keeping track of the minute— i.e., the minutes that the race has been in progress.

For instance, the minute-man might have said just a few seconds ago, "This is the one hundred and fiftieth minute." The second-man on the chronometer is reading, and a recorder picks up Number 87 as the runner crosses the finish line at the 46th second. The recorder writes down on a slip of paper *No. 87-150:46.*

This slip of paper is carried to more recorders who, I hope, are seated at tables in a warm room. If the race has been well organized, these recorders have a card on each racer with the following information (prepared by the secretary while processing entry blanks): name, number, club, and starting time. If these cards are in sequential order it's an easy matter to pull out Number 87's card, record his finish time, make the subtraction, have it checked, and then file the card in another pile of finished racers *according to his position as a finisher.*

### MASS VS INTERVAL STARTS

Now you can see one advantage of a mass start. The recorders know that everyone started at *Zero* minutes, and actually, therefore, the racer's finishing time is his elapsed race time.

**111.** *Fancy scoreboard shows top finishers in the 1984 Olympic 50 km event.*

However, when racers are started at 30-second or one-minute intervals, subtractions are always necessary.

There are other advantages to a mass start:

It's certainly more exciting than the standard interval start.

It's also more practical. If you have a field of 1,000 racers, it would take a long time to get them started, even at 30-second intervals.

Finally, if the watches do fail, *the order of finish after a mass start is the order of finish for the race.*

## CROSS-CHECKS

*Order of finish.* At all races there should be at least one person who records the order of finish. Sometimes the recorders don't have the time to write down both the racers' bib numbers and the time at which they cross the finish line. If the recorder gets the seconds at which the racers cross he then can check with the person who has the numbers of the order of finish, and match them.

**112.** *Start of the prestigious Dusty Ridge Relays, held every year during sugar season in Windham County, Vermont. By invitation only.*

*Back-up watches.* Be sure to have back-up watches. Your chronometer might freeze or stop.

The rules for use of electric timing specify that other watches must be used as back-ups. This makes good sense. The electric timer might malfunction. Or there might be a power failure.

## Food Stations and Refreshments

In long, official races of 30 km and over, the organizers are required to provide food stations for the competitors.

### "OUT OF OUR OWN TEST KITCHENS . . ."

In a short tour race you probably won't need a food station. If you decide to have one, though, or if you want to serve refreshments after the race, I'll give a few popular beverages.

First, though: During a race warm liquids are easiest to swallow. Don't make them too hot. After the race, the temperatures are the dealer's choice.

1. *A word about salt,* which often is added to compensate for excessive loss of body minerals during heavy sweating. We've done this for years without apparent problems, but the latest medical advice indicates this is probably not necessary, or even a good idea. (How did we ever manage before we found this out?)
2. *Equal parts of tea and cranberry juice.* Sugar or dextrose to sweeten.
3. *Tea with lemon and sugar or dextrose.*
4. *Gatorade, Sportade, or some equivalent.*
5. *Any sweet drink made slightly tart with lemon juice*—the extra acidity will cut phlegm build-up, called "cotton mouth."
6. *Weak coffee* with sugar or dextrose.
7. *"Finnish Blueberry Drink,"* prepared as follows: 1 can blueberries, preferably blenderized; 3 cups water; 1 cup sugar; 1 to 2 tablespoons cornstarch. Cook all ingredients except cornstarch to boiling point. Add cornstarch which has been mixed with water. Cook until mixture is thickened. Serve warm.

The skiers should be given advance notice if there is, or isn't, going to be any food for sale after the race.

## Notice, Toilets, Parking

To be safe, you should notify all the local authorities about your race. Include the state police, the sheriff, the selectmen or town officers.

Toilet facilities, *at least* at race HQ, are a must. You know how it is. Chemical or electric toilets—those claustrophobic kiosks now prevalent at construction sites—can be rented. Look under "Toilets, portable" in the Yellow Pages.

Years ago I didn't dream that parking would be a problem at x-c races, but that day has arrived. If you figure one vehicle for every three competitors, even this number can be a sobering thought.

By having the start away from the finish you can split up the parking problem somewhat. This has been a factor in setting courses used for some tour races. Or, if you organized a point-to-point tour, perhaps from one town to another, no one would have to drive anywhere until after the tour. Then you could drive your friends' vehicles back home, where they could jump in and drive to their homes.

## Other Services

### FIRST AID

You should have first-aid provisions, as a minimum. There are plenty of skiing doctors in most x-c areas and often they will volunteer their services or put you on to someone who can cover the race. Or, representatives from a paramedic rescue team from the local fire department may donate their time—in return for a donation to their non-profit organization (this to be regarded as a legitimate race expense).

It's important to have a crew "sweep the trail" at the end of the race. Occasionally a late skier has gotten waylaid and needs help.

### A REFERENCE

Another good reference for race organizers is the manual published by Cross Country Ski Areas of America. Write the association at P.O. Box 557, Brattleboro, Vt. 05301, for information on this booklet.

## That Ounce of Prevention

If you are in charge of a race I've found it's a good drill to sit down after you think everything is in control and let your imagination run rampant. Consider yourself in the role of many different people coming to the race. What will they be apt to want? Are you prepared?

Let's see, there may be coaches, eager parents, pregnant women, nervous grandparents, city folk driving without snow tires, young mothers looking for baby-sitters, well-meaning people who want the sport explained to them in three minutes or less, and so on.

That's not all. If you want to qualify for the ulcer fraternity, go over some of the other, more local possibilities for trouble. (These are all based on my experience and not made up, believe me.)

A landowner calls at minus 12 hours and tells you he has changed his mind about letting the course run over his property.

A soft, gentle rain begins falling on the eve of the race and you've already scraped together all the snow you can find.

The local gendarme shows in the middle of the race and asks, irately, Why all this snow across the road? (He's speaking of the precious stuff that's been hauled in and smoothed to make a track for the skiers.)

Five minutes before the race your friendly road crew comes by and sands all the road crossings.

Your supplier of tea bags discovers, just before the race, that he is out of stock.

The fellow who last used your stopwatches is (a) out of town, or (b) can't find them right now: too busy.

## Then, at the Last Minute—

Your chief timer calls in sick.

Your snow-shovelers can't find shovels and come asking you for some.

Two cars park smack in the middle of a road crossing.

Spectators, eager to see the race, position themselves in the middle of the starting lane.

You prescribe some wax and then there's an eclipse of the sun.

A forerunner comes in and reports that a big tree has just blown down over the track out at the far reaches of the course, and the race is already under way.

The local dog herd engages in a free-for-all in the starting area, wiping out all the tracks and leaving mixed in the snow lots of remains, the least of which is dog hair . . .

Well, what organizer would be without these problems? But your reward comes in knowing how much x-c skiers enjoy any sort of race. It's as simple as that.

# GLOSSARY

**Alpine skiing.** Downhill skiing, named Alpine because of geographic area (Alps) of origin.

**Alpine waxes.** See *Glider* or *Speed waxes*.

**Base waxes.** Usually these are soft Alpine waxes used on *fiberglass* skis to help seal and protect the bottom. Or they can be pine-tar compounds used to help preserve wood skis.

**Binder waxes.** Any wax used to help purchase waxes and speed waxes adhere or last longer; therefore, all binder waxes go on before purchase and speed waxes, and then are covered by them. One of the best-known types of x-c binder is called *Grundvax*.

**Citizens' Race.** Also Citrace, Tour Race, Loppet. Cross-country ski race for large numbers of skiers, of all sizes and shapes. Usually a mass start or a wave start.

**Cork.** The cork used to be a chunk of actual cork for smoothing wax that's been daubed on the ski. However, nowadays a cork is a cork or something synthetic. But at least its use remains the same.

**Corn snow.** Granular snow that has started to melt and therefore is wet. It can be just a trifle moist, or quite wet—depending on the temperature.

**Cushion wax.** A soft wax applied under the foot (the mid-section of the ski) that snow crystals can indent, thereby giving purchase. A cushion is usually covered by another harder, and therefore usually faster, purchase wax. Not used on waxless skis. See also *Kicker zone* and *Purchase waxes*.

**Frozen granular snow.** This is cold, dry, harsh snow that has melted at least once and refrozen. (Westerners refer to it as "Eastern Powder Snow.")

**Glider waxes.** Speed waxes, usually made by x-c wax companies, used on tips and tails.

**Hairies.** The name given to the do-it-yourself waxless skis because of the hairy appearance of the finished base.

**Hard waxes.** Purchase waxes used primarily for powder snow. They come in small "tins" or containers. Before application they give the appearance of being "harder" than klisters.

**Hot-waxing.** The method of ironing speed wax or base wax onto the skis.

**Hypothermia.** A condition in which the body's core temperature drops below 99° F (37° C). In severe cases, death results.

**Iron.** Actually, any piece of metal used, when warmed, to melt and smooth wax. Household irons and special waxing irons are the most commonly seen.

**Kicker zone.** That part of the ski under the foot where purchase wax is applied. Often it is determined by the paper-sliding test for flexibility described in Chapter 1, Equipment. Also called the *kicker strip*.

**Klister snow.** The stuff you use klister wax on—almost always snow that has melted and refrozen. There are two categories under this one: frozen granular snow and corn snow.

**Klister waxes.** Purchase waxes used primarily for granular snow conditions. These waxes come in tubes, are very sticky, and, if you get things messed up just right, can remind you of an underdone taffy-pull.

**Lignostone.** Beechwood compressed and impregnated with resin, used on the edges of skis because of its durability.

**Loppet.** Another name used for Citizens' Race.

**Nordic.** Strictly, all cross-country skiing, biathlon (skiing and shooting) and jumping. So named because of geographic area of origin.

**Orienteering.** Timed race on foot or skis which involves use of map and compass to follow the course.

**Paraffin.** Especially in the U.S.A. and Canada, the soft wax used to seal homemade jellies, etc.; comes in slabs from the supermarket.

**Powder snow.** Until March of '84, something thought by Easterners to occur in North America only in the western part of the continent. Light, fluffy, and soft.

**Purchase waxes.** These are waxes, usually applied to the mid-section of the ski only, that provide purchase, grip or climb. Sometimes referred to as *kicker waxes*.

**Speed waxes.** These are waxes used to make the skis slide easier. Often called *Alpine* or *Glider waxes,* they should be used on tips and tails of waxless skis.

**Spray waxes.** Usually speed waxes, but occasionally purchase waxes, which can be sprayed onto the ski.

I have tried to remain neutral and avoid public announcements about the merits of one ski or any other piece of equipment, or about one touring area or one section of the country that is especially well-suited for cross-country skiing. It's a difficult task. For instance, no sooner does a picture appear in one of my books or articles than someone from a company or a particular area asks me if I am trying to sell something for the "opposition." I get asked if I am in the pay of certain companies and the answer always has been, and still is, "No."

However, every year there is information published on new equipment, old and new ski areas, and many other facets of cross-country skiing. In addition, many authors have different approaches or angles to this sport. In short, there is a lot of other source material that can be read.

Here are my recommendations.

## BOOKS ON CROSS-COUNTRY SKIING

Bengtsson, Hans and George Atkinson. *Orienteering for Sport and Pleasure*, The Stephen Greene Press, 1977.

Brady, Michael. *The Complete Ski Cross-Country: The New Handbook for Touring & Racing*, Doubleday, 1982.

Brady, Michael. *Cross-Country Ski Gear*, Peter Smith, 1983.

Brady, Michael, and Lorns Skjemstad. *Waxing for Cross-Country Skiing*, Wilderness, 1981.

Caldwell, John. *Caldwell on Competitive Cross-Country Skiing*, The Stephen Greene Press, 1979.

Caldwell, John and Michael Brady. *Citizen Racing*, The Mountaineers, 1982.

Diltz-Siler, Barbara. *Understanding Avalanches: A Handbook for Snow Travelers in the Sierra and Cascades*, Signpost Publications, 1977.

Flemmen, Asbjorn and Olav Grosvold. *Teaching Children to Ski*, Human Kinetics, 1983.

Gibb, Henry and Laurie Gibb. *Ski Touring with Kids*, Pruett, 1982.

Gillette, Ned and John Dostal. *Cross-Country Skiing*, The Mountaineers, 1983.

Sharkey, Brian. *Training for Cross-Country Ski Racing*, Human Kinetics, 1984.

Steck, Allen and Lito Tejada-Flores. *Wilderness Skiing*, Sierra Club, 1972.

Tjeda-Flores, Lito. *Backcountry Skiing: The Sierra Club Guide to Skiing Off the Beaten Track*, Sierra, 1981.

## MANUALS

*Avalanche Handbook*, Agriculture Department Handbook #489, U.S. Government Printing Office.

*Cross-Country Citizen Racing—An Organizers Manual*, U.S. Ski Association, 1750 East Boulder St., Colorado Springs, Colorado 80909.

*Operations Manual for Ski Touring Centers*, Cross-Country Ski Areas of America, P.O. Box 557, Brattleboro, Vermont 05301.

*Promoting a Ski Competition*, U.S. Ski Association, 1750 East Boulder St., Colorado Springs, Colorado 80909.

*Swix: Advanced Waxing for Cross-Country Skiing.*

*The Swix Waxing Manual.*

## MAGAZINES

*Cross Country Skier*, Box 1203, Brattleboro, Vermont 05301.

*Skiing*, One Park Avenue, New York, New York 10016.

*Ski X-C*, One Park Avenue, New York, New York 10016.

**113–115.** *Jennifer Caldwell and Howie Bean posed for most of the technique shots on a sunny April day in 1984. Later that afternoon the film crew went back to its sugaring operation.*

# INDEX